I Like to Ride
A TransAmerican Journey

Enjoy the
adventure.

Paul M. S.

I Like to Ride
A TransAmerican Journey

Daniel McDonald

Go Seek Nature
2017

First Printing: 2017

ISBN: 978-0-692-83170-0

Go Seek Nature
Omaha, NE

Visit us at: goseeknature.com

Ordering Information:

Special discounts are available on bulk purchases. For details contact Dan McDonald: dan@goseeknature.com.

U.S trade bookstores and wholesalers: Please also contact Dan McDonald: dan@goseeknature.com.

Dedication

I am forever grateful to my wife Brianne for fully embracing this family adventure across America. To my boys Aaron and Conor I will carry the memories we made always. Thank you mom for being such a wonderful companion to us all along the way.

I would also like to thank all of the great people both in our home town of Omaha and those out in the rural parts of America whom made this truly epic journey possible.

God bless

Contents

I Like to Ride

Chapter 1

The Spark

My first taste of freedom came served on a bicycle. We lived in Phoenix, Arizona then and I had just started the first grade. I soon learned that waiting at the bus stop was not for me. I noticed a boy riding a bicycle down the street towards our elementary school. That looked like the funnest way to get where I was headed and so I ran home to pull my own bicycle from the garage. The world around me grew exponentially that morning.

When we moved to Omaha, Nebraska I sought out the Keystone Trail. It was a couple of miles from our home and curled through the city for miles. My friends and I rode up and down great lengths of the trail as we grew into young adults. I later used the trail as a bicycle highway to the University of Nebraska in Omaha. I had no need for a parking pass during the long years spent as an undergrad of computer science. My wife presented me with a Trek 7000 hybrid bicycle on Christmas morning. It was the best. I soon ventured out far beyond the university and found the trail connected up with another called the Bellevue Loop and that trail led to the river on the far edge of the city.

The years passed and I was content to cycle across the city on the numerous trails and side streets. That all changed when I visited Pittsburg, Kansas on a business trip. We spent the entire morning planning the new infrastructure, the afternoon procuring materials, and all night deploying. We broke for dinner as the dark crept into the poorly lit hallways and settled on a dive Italian restaurant called Napoli's.

I enjoy local food when I travel and the greater the difference from the usual fare the better. Napoli's was an inexpensive restaurant with a college crowd menu consisting of pizza and an assortment of pastas. They served warm bread as you wait for your meal and the food was piled high on large plates. When we pulled into the parking lot my eyes were drawn to a bicycle by the main entrance under a window sill. It was fully loaded with panniers, a sleeping bag, and a tent. I did not know what to make of it, so walked purposefully past it as I entered the building. The aroma of hot melted cheese and tomato sauce piqued my appetite as we settled into our table next to the kitchen. I scanned the restaurant and found the most logical owner of the bike. He was fully bearded and sat behind what had to be two orders of pasta. He was deeply involved with the task at hand. There was a look of peace in his face that you seldom see in our hectic society. This sort of inner quiet certainly had been eluding me for some time. We ate our meal with gusto as usual and then rushed back to our own task at hand.

Later, after our mission was complete, we celebrated by enjoying some booze. The next morning it was time to satisfy my curiosity about the bearded man with the bicycle. Apparently, there was this thing called the TransAmerican Bicycle Trail and it wheeled straight through the town we were in on its way to the Atlantic or Pacific depending upon how you take your prevailing winds. That bearded man was on a glorious and most epic of adventures. I wanted in!

I started to watch videos of other cyclists who had documented their journeys across America. I was beginning to hear the siren's call to lone adventure into the unknown. I broached the subject with my wife one evening and distinctly remember being shot down sharply and quickly. It took three years of bringing it up until she finally relented. There was a catch though. I was not to go alone into the unknown, we all would. I struggled with how this changed my vision of how it would all unfold. I had seen myself alone and unsupported in the wilderness. I also saw the opportunity for a new vision, so we began our plans to journey across the expanse of our great nation together as a family. I am so glad we did.

I Like to Ride

Chapter 2

Preparation

"By failing to prepare you are preparing to fail"
-Benjamin Franklin

I began our preparations by letting my boss know about my intentions to be away from the office for 3 months. Our CEO had just notified the company that she was taking a 90 day paid sabbatical outlined in her benefits. The company was struggling and I imagine that the board was also good with the decision, as it would allow some time to think about the future course of the company. Taking a step back can open one's eyes to all the possibilities.

It was explained to us that we should all be able to take such a sabbatical if our corner of the sandbox was neat and self sustaining. I was glad to hear that. Mine would be unpaid but available to me as outlined in the employee handbook. When the time came to put in the request I was asked to hold off, to think about the loss of pay, and in the end given only 45 days. I was told that the decision had escalated through human resources and then made its rounds in senior leadership before they decided it would set a bad precedent for the other employees. They must have forgotten how driven I was. It was then that my wife and I decided to start saving for my eventual unemployment. I was the Director of Information Technology Services for the company and had a decent paycheck in which to squirrel away over the next six months. We could have saved more as I was still making daily coffee runs but we saved enough. The only debt we had was the mortgage and that could turn into equity pretty quickly as the homes in our neighborhood were selling quickly at ever increasing prices.

Now that work was settled we began looking into what we would need to make the journey. We had ordered some very detailed maps from an organization called Adventure Cycling. Their TransAmerica Trail maps gave us turn by turn directions, milage, elevation changes, local points of interest, and service locations. They were also very weather resistant and folded into handlebar bag sized rectangles. Someone would later tell me that you could even eat them in case of a food emergency! Seriously though, don't try to eat the maps. Go find some edible plants or something.

The maps work even when there is no cell phone service, GPS signal, or when the batteries on your long list of devices have gone dead in the middle of nowhere. They also make great planning material for where and when you will be each day along the journey. The maps were a Christmas gift to ourselves and the stuff my dreams were made of for months.

We purchased an a-frame pop up camper to serve as base camp each night. We had camped through the Rocky Mountains in Colorado the summer before and found that a tent was not going to work very well for our family. We have twin six year old boys and one of our sons has some disabilities. Aaron is a very outgoing boy who shares our love for adventure but also has a tendency to do so on his own terms. He had learned how to open our tent and would try to leave at all hours of the night. We feared he would wander out on a midnight adventure in rural America as we all slept. The camper gave us a layer of protection against things like that as it had a solid door with a lock. Yes, Aaron learned how to use said lock but you can only mitigate the risks so much before you scrap the whole project.

The camper had ample storage for our gear. There was a large storage area under the main bed and several smaller ones throughout. Our model was fittingly called a bike hauler as it had a platform behind the hitch for tying down bicycles, foot lockers, five gallon water jugs, folding chairs, and a pink bucket for grey water. We just might have put more weight up there than we really should have but it held together just fine. Our tow vehicle did squat really low to the ground in the rear though. We also had our tow vehicle for storage. We had purchased the roof rack rails and used the area under the kids feet. We were weighted down to right at or a little over capacity for everything.

Our camper also had a heat pump and microwave for when we were connected to shore power. Shore power is a land power line and ours was 30 amps. We could also run on 20 amps, a standard wall outlet, but at diminished capacity. The camper also had four 20 amp wall outlets for charging our devices and running electrical equipment. We were connected to shore power less than half of our journey and loved the comfort it brought us when we did have it. When we were not connected to the grid we ran on a deep cycle lead acid battery. The battery was able to run an attic fan, lights, water pump, refrigerator, and thermostat for our propane heater. There was the aforementioned heater for keeping us warm on cold summit nights and a propane stove for cooking the vast majority of our meals. The battery charged off the tow vehicle during daily hops between camp sites and this was sufficient because we moved pretty much every day. We also had a solar panel for charging while stationary but only used it once. Not because our battery was low but just to try it out.

The camper had two beds. A large full time queen sized bed and a convertible kitchen table that turned into a full. The queen had a good mattress that had a heated blanket built into it for what I could only imagine would be one heck of a cold night as the heat pump worked well down into the 30's. The propane heater worked even better in the dead of the night but eats into the gas supply. We had two grill sized propane tanks in the front of the camper on the hitch right behind the battery and they lasted the entire trip.

There was also a 16 gallon fresh water tank, water pump, and shore water connection. We carried a lot of water with us and had access to it through the battery and pump when we were off grid. The tank was under the camper and this offered it shade from the sun leaving it cooler than it would have been otherwise. We also carried a five gallon water jug on the bike hauler for easy access during the day when the camper was folded up. The camper does fold back up in about a minute but having extra water within hands reach is always nice.

The trailer that the camper was built on had a single axle with four stabilizing jacks for deployment while stationary. The hitch runs off of the battery and had a manual crank in the event that the battery was drained. The side walls and roof of the camper deployed with the aid of hydraulic arms making it very easy to set up and take down. Ample LED lighting was run outside and in for use on or off shore power. There were smoked glass windows and plexiglass skylights allowing for ample daytime light and a cross breeze when the attic fan was running.

Our tow vehicle was wired to tow small trailers without trailer brakes. Our trailer had brakes, power needs, and lights. I spent a great deal of time researching how to wire the SUV and then purchased the necessary materials for the job at our local Walmart. It took me about four hours of labor to tear down the vehicle's interior, find a path for the wires, open the fire wall between the driver and the engine compartment, and then install the necessary breakers, wires, and fuses. The original brake controller I purchased was time delayed and I hated it. It would start soft and then ratchet up the braking until it hit a preset limit. It then would stay on until you released the pedal. This caused it to hum loudly at stops and you could tell you were towing a heavy trailer behind you. Thankfully Brianne accidentally kicked the controller off of its face while getting into the vehicle one day. I switched it out for the more advanced version.

I ride a Trek 7000 bicycle, my main source of transportation for the summer. It was unfortunately in great need of an overhaul before undertaking such a journey as this. I had been riding it for many years and had changed out the wheels, tires, inner tubes, chain, rear cassette, and bottom bracket on other occasions but it was time for almost all brand new components. I began by researching what they were putting on the newer model of Trek hybrids and then worked through what would work on my bicycle. I ordered the parts online from Amazon in order to get the most bang for my buck and set to rebuilding her over the winter. I used Google and YouTube to learn how to make brake and shifter cables. The process was a bit tedious at first as I had never done it before but the final product turned out great! With new cables, shifters, brake components, and brake pads the bike stopped on a dime and shifted like a dream. I also changed out the bottom bracket, both front and rear derailleurs, the front crank, rear cassette, chain, handlebar grips, and made repairs to the brazens which held the water bottles and rear rack in place. One of the old brazens fell into the frame as I worked it off and still rattles there to this day. I replaced my clip-in pedals and then the clips on my bicycle sandals. I also purchased two sets of most components for re-placement in Pueblo, Colorado, the half way point on the tour. The bicycle was now in tip top shape and I was proud of my handy work.

I rode all through the winter both outdoors and in a spin class at the local YMCA. I trained hard but was careful not to test the injury gods who like to strike those who over train. I loved the spin classes. Brianne had introduced them to me as a fun way to spend my training hours at the gym. I worked real-ly hard to prepare myself for the mountains and continuous cranking I would endure all summer long. I would later dis-cover that hitting the stair stepper might have been a good idea too as the mountain ascents felt like hours of stair climbing.

I dieted to drop weight in order to make my spokes last longer, I tend to break a lot of spokes, and to increase my over-all speed. I weighed in at 280 pounds the evening before the first day of pedaling and weighed around 300 before the diet-ing. You might think that I am a little crazy to attempt such an adventure at 280 to 300 pounds but I am a big man and carry a good deal of muscle to go with my well earned waistline! I changed my diet to vegan which was made easier by already being a vegetarian. There are a few traps that you can fall into with this diet as there are many refined foods that you are able to eat but should not. I did this for six months before leaving and went back to eating milk, cheese, and eggs the day we headed out for the East Coast. I love dairy and eggs. It was so good to be vegetarian again.

So why am I a vegetarian you might ask? It keeps my blood pressure down naturally. I had started to see my blood pressure rise over the years and was even put on beta blockers at one point. I hated those pills and switched doctors to someone who was more willing to help me achieve balance without medicine. I was able to keep between prehypertensive and stage one for around five years with lifestyle changes but was unable to get it back to normal until Brianne had me try the vegetarian diet. I have no issues with eating animals and was even a butcher for several years but I agreed because I love my wife and she gets her way. The damnedest thing happened though after just one week of eating no meat. I had an eye doctor appointment, they screen your blood pressure nowadays, and I warned the technician that it would be elevated. She laughed at me and said it was 120/80. Well, hot damn it had been years since it had ever read that low. I was not entirely convinced though and waited a few more months as a vegetarian before getting my annual check up and discovering that this was my cure. I like to tell people that everyone is different but hey, give it a shot if you have hypertension as it might just be the cure for you too.

So there I was, down 20 pounds and in good cardiovascular health when May rolled around. I wish I could say that I had trained enough but I do not believe that you can ever be fully prepared for such a test of endurance and spirit as a summer of riding 65 to 110 miles per day for 66 days. We took 5 days off in total but riding my bicycle became a way of life.

We also needed to pack dry goods for the journey as we would be feeding a family of four and our 107 pound black lab Gabriel, who we affectionally call black bear. Our boys had started to eat more and more as they began growing at a furious pace. I would be burning thousands of calories a day. We hit up the usual bulk goods markets in town and packed two foot lockers full of pasta, rice, canned goods, macaroni & cheese, grape seed oil, oatmeal, grits, powdered milk, potato flakes, and seasonings. With the easy carbohydrates taken care of we planned on getting our vitamins and minerals from local produce as we traveled across the states. I had gotten our dry goods list off of a church website which broke down what a family of four would need to survive on for three months, should the need arise. Well, the need had arisen, it had arisen indeed!

So we were prepared. We had our maps, home, vehicle, bicycle, food, clothing, parts, tools, toys, books, technology, and a good idea of how we were going to go about this epic adventure. I waited until 30 days before we had planned on hitting the road and gave my resignation at work. It was a hard decision to make because I really enjoyed what I had accomplished there over the last decade and my coworkers were really just plainly put, my friends. The company had changed though and I did not see myself as a part of what it was on its way to becoming. It was time to part ways and I did just that closing this chapter of my life while sprinting headlong into the next as I often do once every decade. Good bye old ways and hello open road!

I Like to Ride

Chapter 3

You Have to Start Somewhere

The camper and the SUV were all packed. I resigned from my job and worked through the last 30 days as a Director of Information Technology Services. We pulled the kids a week early from school and closed up the house for the summer. There was enough money in our savings to travel for 90 days and return to our home with a few months to look for another source of income. It was time to go and we said our goodbyes to our family and friends.

We planned on stopping in North Carolina to visit Brianne's grandparents and her uncle Jeff before driving up to Yorktown, Virginia where the ride traditionally starts. It was early May and the weather was still bordering on cool to warm as it transitioned into summer. We pulled out of the driveway with our heavily loaded camper, scraping the hitch as we sailed out into the adventure of a lifetime. Everything had greened up as spring progressed and I lamented not being able to plant our annual garden. I had thought about planting some things like pumpkins or sunflowers in hopes that nature would look after them in our absence but decided against it at the last moment. Now we were gone and that was that for the garden this year. We had planned on traveling through the day and into the evening making our way to the Daniel Boone Conservation Area just outside of St Louis, Missouri. It was to be our first night of boondocking, camping in a recreational vehicle for free, and we were both excited and nervous. I was eager to get to riding my bicycle too and had to temper my excitement just for a few more days.

Our first round of unexpected excitement came in the form of camper trouble. We were a good hour or so down the road when I drove over a metal object in the center of our lane. It looked like something I could clear with ease and it might well have been if I were not hauling a fully loaded camper. Our trailer's brakes locked up moments after passing the object and we were rudely jolted into a forced deceleration as the camper dragged behind. I quickly pulled us off onto the shoulder and got out to survey the possible damage. Cars whizzed past me as I made my way back to the camper. I did a walk around as they had taught us in the Army and checked for foreign objects, tire trouble, brake issues, and came across nothing. I was puzzled for a long moment before it hit me. The metal object had knocked out the emergency trailer brake plug and those crazy brakes had done just what they were built to do in case of an emergency separation of the tow vehicle at high speeds! Well, unfortunately, or fortunately, this was not the case and we ended up dragging some dead weight for an eighth of a mile. The good news was that the problem was instantly resolved and there was no noticeable damage done to the vehicle or the camper. Soon we were on the road again and a little wiser to boot.

Our next issue came as a warning notice on our SUV dash. We had purchased new tires before leaving town and the shop had a lot of trouble replacing the automatic tire pressure sensor gauges in all four of the tires. Well, they failed on day one and began alerting us that day and just about every day for Brianne after that. I was worried about it at first but quickly chalked it up to a "nice to have fixed" verses a "must repair now show stopper." The rest of our travels to the conservation area were less eventful and we were thankful for that.

It was late when we left the interstate for the backroads. We had not really put much thought into why these places would be free to park a trailer at overnight but we began to learn that evening how off the beaten path they tend to be. The paved road ended just past an old church in the middle of nowhere. It was dark and there were no natural or artificial lights to guide our way. The moon was of no help as it was hidden away by the clouds. Our SUV had developed some headlight challenges as a result of the film that built up on the light covers over the years. The dirt road stretched on into the pitch black night. It became narrower and bumpier with every passing mile. It even began to wind up a grade as we approached where the GPS was telling us would be camping for the night. We wondered aloud to each other if there would be others out here or just us. We had a vague description of what the site looked like from an app about dispersed campsites on my phone but it was hard to tell if we had reached it as there were several severely degrad- ed side paths along the road we were on. We had passed the welcome sign to the conservation area though and knew we were almost there. I do not remember arguing with Brianne as we searched for what felt like forever in the dark for a place to park but I imagine we might have as couples often do on long road trips when they are tired and not sure about the right path forward.

The road began to washboard and we had to avoid several large potholes where the dirt and gravel had eroded but we came across what had to be what we had read about on the app. There, cut into the trees, were several paths that recreational vehicles much larger than our camper could fit comfortably into. I pulled the vehicle around a few trees and lined us up for a straight shot at the road should we need to exit hastily in the middle of what was left of the night.

Brianne and I jumped out of the SUV to start setting up camp while the kids waited nervously in their seats. Conor tends to get a little out of sorts in situations like these where he is left in the vehicle for a time in the dark not knowing what we are doing or when we will come back for him. There was a time the summer before when we had come to our camp site at Lake McConaughy, in Western Nebraska, around 11PM and had to set up our tent in the not so great light of our SUV headlights. It was a rough experience with Conor yelling out for us in near tears as we fumbled with our tent poles, rainfly, and stakes. This time around he did not have to wait nearly as long as our camper is quick and easy to deploy. I did not bother unhitching as we were just going to drive on in the morning so I put the tongue jack down to relieve some pressure on the rear suspension of the SUV and deployed the four stabilizing jacks underneath into the semi-muddy ground. Brianne opened up the camper and deployed the side walls. She locked them down at each corner and then turned on the attic fan to pull air through the screened windows. We were all hot and sweaty from the muggy night air and our hurried labor to get camp setup. I turned on the propane and Brianne got the children along with Gabriel into the camper. She cooked dinner as I locked things up for the night. We ate quickly, turned out the lights, and lay in a pool of our sweat wondering what the night would bring out here in this place where we were the only souls around for miles.

We may not have slept much but the night was really peaceful other than the boogie men our minds might have concocted about the place we had made home for the evening. The morning light revealed a beautiful landscape dense with forest, wild flowers, birds, squirrels, and box turtles. Brianne cooked a vegetarian skillet and we had a hearty breakfast before venturing out into the surrounding woods to explore. Later I fixed up a few broken spokes on my bicycle and finished preparing it for game day! Our adventure sure was off to a good start. There had already been unexpected surprises, warning lights, boondocking for the first time in a conservation area, and exploration. We were just getting started.

We headed out of the conservation area before lunch and came across several box turtles and abandoned cabins on the way out. Of course we stopped and took pictures of everything we saw. It was a great experience and I would recommend it to anyone passing through. The weather was warmer and humid during the day's drive and the air conditioning stopped blowing cold air at one point. I had filled the Freon before we left to avoid such a scenario and was a bit concerned that Brianne and the boys would be without cool air this summer. We stopped at a rest area and I propped open the hood. I was very surprised to see a frozen block of metal in the engine compartment near the fire wall. I guess I might have added a little too much Freon or it was just that kind of weather where things could freeze up like this. We waited for it to melt as we ate lunch at a picnic table and the air went back to full on cold as we drove back out onto the interstate.

Our next vehicle excitement came in the form of a flapping storage door on the rear right of the camper. My favorite back-pack along with most of my riding clothing dodged a bullet here as they were precariously close to falling out over lord knows how many miles. I quickly ascertained that the bolt holding the locking mechanism in place had worked itself loose as we cruised down the road. No doubt our off road adventure the evening before had something to do with this turn of events. I walked over to the other storage door to the front of the right side of the camper and produced my tool kit. I took hold of my Philips head screw driver and fixed that issue in a jiffy!

The rest of the day's drive was long and we started to pull into the Daniel Boon National Forest at dusk. The forest was beautiful in the orange glow of the setting sun. There was a lake and the area felt good to be in. We followed our GPS up steep and winding grades along the way to where we had re-searched a dispersed campsite on a side road. Dispersed camp-ing is both free and perfectly fine in National Forests and we had planned to make use of this little known fact all the way across America. What we did not account for was how difficult this could prove to be in most National Forests. Our dispersed campsite app had described this site as a little seedy. We were wary of putting our children into a seedy situation for the evening but had some confidence from the night before. Well, I guess the Forest Service did not like the seediness of the site and had closed the road to it at some point. We found this out a little too late as we ended up facing a barricade on a one lane road with nowhere to turn a camper around. Brianne and I worked together to back out and crank ourselves around. The sun was nearly set as we began to backtrack to a designated pay site we had passed on the way to the dead-end road. Brianne was disappointed with her goal being to camp for free as often as possible but it did have water and power which made our evening a lot more comfortable. Dinner was awesome and we both agreed that it was nice to have a solid place to call home that night. The good news was that we only paid half the price, since camping in National Forests is discounted due to Aaron's lifetime disability.

Aaron was born with a little known and early onset form of infantile epilepsy called Ohtahara Syndrome. It presents with burst suppression readings on an EEG. For Aaron this meant having upwards of 300 seizures per day. He would awake, we would feed him, he would seize uncontrollably, throw-up, and pass out. The first hospital sent him to another hospital where they sent him home to pass on. We could not accept this outcome for our new baby boy and took him to a children's hospital where, by the grace of God, a pediatric neurologist knew exactly what was wrong and sent us with hope to Minnesota where they operated on his brain to separate the two hemispheres. The left separated from the right, so he could live seizure-free using only his good right hemisphere. The long term prognosis is unknown for him but better than the two years of torturous life predicted for him originally. He is partially paralyzed on his right side and is nonverbal. There are some challenges involved in embarking on such an epic adventure with his unique set of disabilities but totally worth it!

The next day we drove through West Virginia which is beautiful but full of tolls along the way. They detracted from its beauty for us as we shelled out our savings just to drive through the state. We finally arrived in North Carolina that evening. Seeing family there was the best. Brianne's grandmother had picked fresh strawberries with Jeff and we ate them before supper. We spoke of the journey ahead of us and caught up on everyones' year. We always love coming to North Carolina where the people are great and there is so much to do. Brianne's grandparents' church put us up for two nights in their back parking lot giving us access to their power. It was a well lit area tucked away from the road. Having air conditioning every evening was truly a blessing. We thanked the pastor on the way out and stopped at my favorite breakfast place in the area, Biscuitville.

Fully loaded on love, coffee, scrambled eggs, and yummy biscuits we headed out for Yorktown, Virginia where this crazy adventure would really begin to get underway.

Chapter 4

An Account

I did my best to keep a daily journal of my bicycle travels. I mostly succeeded, especially in the beginning, but got lost in the journey towards the end. My mind began to drift with the days and the long miles. The need to record the details became a casualty of my new life on the road.

The ride traditionally starts, when going from East to West, in Yorktown, Virginia at the Yorktown Monument. The area is really neat as it gives the rider an opportunity to slowly pedal through the colonies on their way out into the rural Virginia countryside. The monument itself is tall and fitting for the beginning of such an epic journey. I recommend starting at dawn basking in the first rays of morning light as you touch the cold stone of the monument before heading out into the unknown. The path curls around a short span of Main Street and whooshes down Comte De Grasse Street to the water on the aptly named Water Street. There might be an old wooden ship docked at the marina as you pass by. The sun will begin to pour out onto you now with all of its morning glory, if the sky is clear of course. You will venture onto the Colonial Parkway from there, which is paved with large slabs of stone. This parkway, while steeped in history, can be hard on your spokes if you are a more heavily weighted rider such as myself. Do not worry if things shake loose or break down in the first 20 to 30 miles as you have so much more glorious adventure ahead of you. Nothing can spoil it for you now that you are underway!

I Like to Ride

On the subject of repairs I have this advice to offer heavier riders. Take a spoke wrench, spokes, spoke nipples, spare inner tubes, tire pump, tire lever, chain whip, cassette lock-ring removal tool, and crescent wrench. I know, it is a tall order to add this spoke replacement kit to your pack as it will weigh you down a bit more but I used this kit at least 26 times while on the road and found it very helpful in the middle of nowhere on boiling hot summer days without shade or assistance anywhere in sight. Did I forget to mention your cell phone will be out of range for services when all of this goes down too? Practice your technique at home a couple of times and if you have anything close to my experience with your spokes along the route you will be swapping them out in minutes. Trust and believe that every minute will count as the mosquitos get the message that dinner is served.

Daniel McDonald

Virginia

God smiled down upon our journey with morning light.
The sun's full frontal assault on the day curled around the

church in all of its magnificent glory. The journey ahead truly did feel blessed.

A full and brilliant rainbow the evening before had drawn us out onto the wet grass in the yard behind the cycling ministry's home for fellow travelers. A woman named Amy who we had just met joined us. The kids ran around shirtless and barefoot as I looked up to the heavens and Brianne captured the moment on our digital camera. The yard rested above a river walk and sandy beach which touched the mouth of the York River, which in turn spilled out into the Atlantic ocean. There was a sign on a pathway to the side of the yard warning cyclists to stay off the private walkway adjacent to the home next door. I imagine the owner of that home did not like to share their prime real estate with the multitudes of travelers who made this journey each year. I wondered how different their lives might be if they were open to sharing in the rich tales that such travelers could bring them from the West. We walked back into the home and Brianne cooked dinner as the boys and I explored the old place. There were journals and pictures of those who had come before us to pore over while we waited. Aaron tried to go up and down the steep staircase that led to the upper rooms but I continuously blocked his passage to avoid an injury on the eve of our departure. The upstairs rooms were well kept with carefully made beds and windows facing out to the river. The boys and I showered and then I chased them around one of the rooms to dress them. They had a bit of sand in their shoes from our walk earlier down by the water. It reminded me of the sand that Aaron poured out onto my chain and rear cassette while we took pictures of my rear tire dip. It is tradition for a cyclist to dip the rear tire in a body of water before they began such a journey as I was about to. The journey would then end with a dip of the front tire in the body of water at its completion. I was so cross with Aaron at the time and would come to know it was futile to care about dirty components on my bicycle as I would be subjecting it to much worse in the months to come. Conor too would later pour sand into my drive train on a beach on the Pacific ocean and by then I would not care at all. So I felt sorry for being so cross with Aaron now as he delighted in his christening of my bicycle with sand.

We came down stairs for dinner and sat at the wooden table in the dining room. Amy had her bike parked in the room and I admired it from my chair. It was a sturdy road bike set up for trekking long distances complete with a Brooks saddle, which from what I have been told is the most comfortable seat on the market. I was riding a hybrid bicycle with a seat that I had picked out to replace my last stock seat and it was chosen for low cost but durability in all types of weather. I like to ride in the rain, snow, sun, and you name it types of weather. One year I played around with how cold of a morning ride I could tolerate and rode 14 miles in negative 33 degree windchill. It had been very windy, cold, and my skin burned as it came back to life in my hot morning shower. Amy's bicycle was forest green and looked like a great ride for a cross country journey. I felt confident in my choice of ride too because I had rebuilt all but the frame over the winter and it was a gift from Brianne. I had also already ridden it across Iowa and Nebraska. The Des Moines Register had been putting on a cross state ride through Iowa since 1973 called RAGBRAI which stands for Register's Annual Great Bike Ride Across Iowa. I rode in the 2014 ride to see if I would even make it through one state. I rode in BRAN, Bike Ride Across Nebraska, in 2015 because the time was not right to do the whole country.

Dinner came out and was heavy on the carbohydrates! Brianne had made pasta with peas mixed in. I ate as much as my stomach would hold as I was familiar with what an entire day of pedaling would do to my energy stores. After dinner we walked back up to the camper which was parked at the front of the Grace Episcopal Church. Our camper, that Brianne had named Isosceles, was parked right up against the pine trees with the front door looking out over a beautiful garden that led up to the church. We had been greeted by John earlier who ran the ministry and he made us feel most welcome.

Brianne went back to the home by the river to shower as the boys and I prepared for bed. The sun was setting and the light was all but gone for the day. Aaron was playing in the grass in front of the camper with a toy he had dug out of a storage compartment under the bed nearest the door. He was getting a little grass stained in the damp evening but was so content I let him carry on. Conor requested a ghost story and I wove a short tale of a zombie raccoon who comes to scratch at a camper not unlike ours in the middle of the night. The raccoon nearly has its way with the family inside but a protective Black Lab saves the family as they sleep. No one is the wiser and they all live happily ever after until the next ghost story and there were many to come.

I was struck by the kindness of this church and their ministry as I drifted off to sleep in our home away from home. Brianne had returned and we were all snuggled in for the night making use of the two beds Isosceles had to offer. We were warm, cozy, full, safe, and content.

The monument was a great place to start as it towered over us like the journey ahead. I came across a sushi restaurant on the beach as I rolled down Water Street and took a picture on my phone for some friends back in Omaha who I used to dine with on all sorts of beautifully crafted sushi. I took my first wrong turn of the trip a little down the road and discovered a bamboo forest. I had never seen one so large and extensive. It sounded peaceful as each stock swayed in the water front breeze of the morning. Another wrong turn led me to a red brick bridge arching over the road. I took a short video of my travel underneath and then quickly turned around to get back on the right track. I came across a dark tunnel with a sign warning pedestrians and cyclists to stay out so I went around and found myself in colonial Williamsburg. I walked the bicycle for a stretch on the gravel and then pedaled through old streets with horse drawn carriages. I did my best to work myself around to where the tunnel should have spilled back out into the light of day but alas ended up where I started facing the tunnel again. I took this as a sign that I was meant to venture through the unknown dark and stopped to don my lights. Away I went into the dark. The tunnel was not so bad after all as there was no traffic on my way through and my front light shown brightly against the walls lighting everything up in my path. On the other side of the tunnel I exited more sure of myself and happy with my selection in lighting.

Lunch with the family was at a park by a large river a few more hours down the path. I was ravenous and a little worn out from the fresh air or more aptly the head wind I had been pushing through. A trail had replaced the highway and stretched out for 34 miles. I was happy to be with my family again and soon had my fill of pickles, chips, fresh fruit, and peanut butter sandwiches. I had left about an hour earlier than Amy and rode out of the park's parking lot passing her on my way back down the path. She had stopped in at the same spot to break for lunch too and we said a quick hello. I was off again onto the trail and had many more miles to cover before the end of the day. The smell of pine flowed in and out of my nostrils as I pedaled into the forest. The wind in the trees made the day just about as serene as it could have been. I rode on for some time and eventually came across a side road leading into a small town along the route. I stopped at their post office to rest and sat in silence as I watched the patrons sipping coffee and tea under umbrellas at the shop across the street. I was too hot and sweaty to want to join them and so there I sat letting my mind and body drift into a semi nap out of the sun. I was getting increasingly worn out at this point and had to force myself up again 30 minutes later. My legs were stiff now and I worked them into submission before picking the bike up and placing it back upon the road just off the curb. I was off again.

The ride was harder through the afternoon as I began to double what had been my usual training miles. Then there were the hills on the way to the church where we were to spend the night. I passed families with their children out on the path and then a pile of hand carried rocks where the path ended. I took these as a totem of those who had completed all of its miles from start to finish. I wondered how many of those who had ridden up to here had just kept going until they reached the other coast? I was really tired now. The day had its way with me with the two broken spokes, headwind, sun, and more miles than I was used to. Willis Church Road repeated through my mind as I cranked out the final strokes of the day. The church we were to stay at was on this road and I knew that once I was on it I was almost home. It did finally come but not until the road started to pitch uphill challenging me even more. I struggled past cannons set out on a field as they must have been back during the Revolutionary War. Just a few more miles took me to an opening in the trees at a T in the road where I could see the church up ahead. The light of the day was fading and it was a good time to check in. Brianne cheered me on as I rode into the parking lot. She had deployed the camper already and it sat in front of the church off to the right of the entrance. There was power and we had the run of the kitchen, showers, dining hall, and children's area inside. There was a small playground outside and a picnic table. I ran around with the boys on the playground as Brianne cooked dinner in the kitchen. A man rode his bicycle into the parking lot and stopped by the entrance looking around. I let him know about the amenities offered to cyclists here and he introduced himself as Micheal. Conor instantly took a liking to him as he shared almost all of his chips with him. Michael was from Washington State and he was heading westbound like us. We had both gone 65 miles the first day. He had done so because of a late start though and I had taken a full day to get there. About an hour later Amy showed up too and we all talked about our day before heading to our respective homes for the night. We slept in Isosceles while Amy took the children's play area. Micheal took up residence in a meeting room down the hall. What a great start the day had been in our journeys.

The morning air was brisk and stung my exposed skin as I was not wearing my jacket. I could see my breath as I pedaled through the dawn. It puffed out of me as I exhaled and then it was gone. An early start to the day with no wind to hold me back allowed me to push far down the road with ease. At mile 17 I broke my third spoke. I was now beginning to realize that this would be a daily chore as I rode on the "off the shelf" wheel I had purchased before heading out of Omaha. It would be up until I had replaced the weaker spokes at least and there were 36 of them, well 33 to go now. The old wheel really needed rebuilding. I had never built a wheel before, but had ordered all of the spokes and the new hub that I would need to do so along the way. I had become most proficient at changing out broken spokes though and this made me happier with my circumstances.

Morning rush hour was lighter out in the more rural part of the coast and the road felt safer than it did the day before where cars passed me at a steady pace all day until I was on the long separate path. I came off a back country road and into a larger commercial area of sorts. There I spotted Dunkin Donuts and was delighted to stop in for coffee and 1,000 glorious calories of raised dough topped with sugar. The map looked off as I studied it from my perch outside of the shop. It took me a moment but I found that I had ridden onto another map section. This was a pleasant surprise!

The halfway point for the day, as decided upon last night after dinner, was a park in Charles City and I rode in around 10AM. It was a tad bit early for lunch though. Brianne and the boys were out getting supplies and I napped on a picnic table as the sun moved in and out of intensity behind the foliage of the trees. The rest was great and later when my family arrived the lunch was grander still! A Coke, Fritos, peanut butter with honey sandwiches, blueberries, pickles, and bananas. Aaron and Conor played on the playground while Brianne and I caught up. She had begun to settle in well to our new way of life on the road and this made me happy. I wanted her to enjoy this experience as much as I was.

After a long rest and my fill of good food I took off again ready to tackle the afternoon. I headed down the road and ended up along train tracks dividing a main street. I cruised past shops and had to take many turns on my way out of town. Then I was on the backroads again and they were dotted here and there with mean spirited hills. I found my easiest of gears brought me no comfort and this was a dark omen as the Appalachian Mountains awaited me in a day or two. I was truly exhausted as I reached a giant but beautiful lake. The traffic was heavy here and the route took me out of the way in order to give me a glimpse of this magnificent area. I later found that Amy had detoured past the lake loop taking the most direct route through the area and part of me thought that was the better way but I also feel that experiencing the lake was part of the journey as well.

My lungs began to complain with every breath as I climbed up and down the hills on the road around the lake. I found an old Lions Club park to sleep in a while and dreamt of the days when I first returned from the war in Iraq. I was younger back then and in better shape for such a hilly adventure as this. I grimaced a little as I hopped back on the saddle and rode off into the late afternoon. My pace had slowed to 8 mph and I found out that there was not much left to give. At 80 miles I was ready to be done, but still I rode on past abandoned homes and burning trash piles in the front yards of the occupied ones. My lungs screamed at me as I climbed the final evil sets of hills into the town of Mineral where my family had set up camp in a vacant bluegrass festival park. I crossed a Mexican restaurant as I crested the final hill for the day. It was on the way to the park and the smell of tacos lofted about in the evening air. Oh boy did I want a taco! I would have also wanted to have a pitcher of margaritas. Lime please with salt around the rim. All the salt ya got por favor.

My family was down by the main stage of the vacant blue-grass festival park as I limped in on the gravel road. Isosceles invited me to sit awhile and I said yes. There was a half finished bottle of water inside and I happily report it was quickly and completely emptied, but then again so was I.

The boys and Brianne gave me lots of hugs and kisses. She cooked sweet and sour stir fry for dinner as I sipped Turkish coffee with cream outside on a picnic table. Conor wanted another round of ghost stories and I expanded upon my zombie animal repertoire for him. We played Candyland after supper and relaxed as the sun started to set for the evening. Amy rolled in just about then and we all caught up with each other. I could tell Brianne enjoyed the additional adult company and I was happy for her. We spoke of the next day to come and found it to be another 70 plus mile push to stick with our schedule. We rescheduled and it became a 56 mile day. I helped Amy set up her tent as the light left the sky. She warned us of the rainy day we had to ride through tomorrow and I resolved myself to awake early again. We all slept. Gabriel woke me at 5AM like clock work as he likes to do.

The morning started grey and wet with drizzling rain. I quickly set to packing my bike for the day and said my good-byes. Amy was still asleep in her tent as I ventured out. I coasted down the dirt road past the festival's vacant grand stand and then up a slightly steep hill before popping up over the curve onto the paved street that led to the main one and ultimately out of town.

The rush of cars and school buses passed me by as I meandered through the increasing intensity of what would soon be a downpour. The road turned off to the right into the backcountry and I was lost in time as the rain completely soaked me and the trees closed in on both sides of the road. The smell of wet pine filled the air and I breathed it in deeply. There were small cottages and homesteads along the path with smoke wisping from their chimneys up and out into the dreary sky.

Lunch was gas station nachos topped with orange salt and a warm cup of joe. I had parked my bicycle outside the overhang in front of the small shop and removed my sopping helmet and jacket before entering. There was nothing that could be done about the lake I now introduced to the tile floor and the clerk looked up at me and said, "I know it's raining out there." He went back to looking down at his magazine and I moved about the store looking for said nachos and hot coffee. I really needed a salty carb filled snack along with caffeinated warmth to ease the nature of the day in my soul. I ate my lunch outside to avoid turning the lake into an ocean. A few customers pulled in and out of the fuel pumps giving me searching glances. I must have been a sight. My lunch hit the spot and I saddled up getting back on the way to Charlottesville.

The city reintroduced me to what it is like to cycle through congested traffic and I soon took a wrong turn down a long hill. You would think that I would have been a little more keen about double checking the right path forward before descending such a long steep hill in heavy traffic but hey I was still getting the hang of this. Perhaps it was meant to be though as I caught up with Michael at a statue in the middle of the road in downtown Charlottesville. He was in front of this grand statue to something or other and I rolled through the dense traffic to meet him. We talked for about 15 minutes before moving on to a Starbucks down the road at the university. We propped our bicycles outside against the stone building and headed into the warmth. We waited in line breathing in the alluring smell of fresh ground roasted beans. I swear the smell does more for me than the beverage. Sometimes I just bury my face in a fresh bag of coffee before I finally spoon it out into my current method of steeping this magic in a cup. I thanked the woman behind the counter for my coffee and worked my way over to the doctoring station which was full of cream and spices. There I ladled on the heavy cream and poured in ounce after ounce of sugar. Micheal's bike fell over as he came up beside me. I was staring out of the window into the wet street and he ran out to right it. I should have helped him but I was a bit of a zombie there for a moment holding that warm cup of invigoration. We decided to move on to Afton after about 45 minutes. Afton was what I would call the gateway to the Appalachian Mountains, if you are heading westbound that is. There is a home there affectionally referred to by fellow travelers as the cookie lady's house. The woman had passed into legend a few years back and the home remained as a refuge to cyclists along the path. It was to be a shock of an uphill climb to reach it, for a man like me from Nebraska, but hey what else was there to do.

I met up with Brianne and the boys at a tractor supply operation just outside of Charlottesville and received an 8 mm Allen wrench to fix my wobbly left pedal. My crank bolt had come loose while pedaling endlessly through the rain that day and it was getting close to unridable. I had not thought I would need the larger wrench for the crank but now I would be carrying it always as that thing would come loose just about every time it rained from there until the West Coast. That annoying issue had been causing me to stop every mile or so to kinda tighten it with a 6 mm Alan wrench which was very difficult to do as you might imagine. I ate peanut butter and honey sandwiches while Brianne restocked my water bottles. It was really good to see my family, top off on sustenance, and to have the tools I needed to ride on. I was soon off again. It did not rain much in the evening but became progressively colder as I began to climb into the foot hills of the mountains. The hills became unkind and just as I completed what was to be the last of them for the night I took a left when I should have gone right. This wrong turn before checking my route trouble I was having got rectified after this event, for the most part that is. I rode down hill at 30 mph for two miles before I realized what I had done and slammed on the brakes in a quick panic. The bike came screeching to a halt in front of someone's driveway. I got out my phone and consulted Google Maps which was less help than one would think in these parts. I had just added another 30 minutes of climb to my day. I rode my weary body up the steep climb once more and stopped to walk from time to time.

I Like to Ride

It was divine to again summit that hill and limp into the cookie lady's home. I stood outside and took my picture though before entering for the night. Isosceles was parked an inch off the road in the dirt next to the home which was itself only a foot from the road. I heard a voice from behind questioning me, "Are you going to sleep in that camper tonight?" I turned around to meet a man who had walked up the driveway across the road to speak with me. I let him know I would be sleeping indoors tonight and he thought that was a good idea as there was a bear lurking around these parts the last few days getting into things. I thanked him and entered the old home. Brianne had made a hardy vegetable barley soup and it warmed my sopping cold wet soul right up. Micheal was in the other room with Gabriel curled up next to him on an old dusty coach. He had found a fan to dry his shoes off in front of and I made use of it as well. No sense in having wet feet all day tomorrow too if it could be helped. The rest room had a sign above the toilet warning the user not to flush too many times as it was on a septic system that overfilled easily. I made a mental note to keep Aaron out of there as he loves to flush toilets to no end. The home was spread out with keep sakes from decades of travelers who had left their totems on the way through. Brianne found a list of places we could stay at later in Kentucky along with phone numbers which all proved to be so old that the residence had moved on since leaving their calling cards. There was even a phone number for a gentlemen who would come with his pickup truck and toss your bike in the back as he spirited you over the Blue Ridge Parkway and into Kentucky. I do not think anything less of those who would wish his services as their journeys are their own to take but I wanted to feel every inch of this adventure.

I fell asleep holding Aaron in my arms later after tucking Conor into a semi-swaddle on the couch in the living room. The light of morning awoke me as it snuck in through the windows above the couch. It would be a day of nothing but climbing as I ascended the Blue Ridge Parkway.

The parkway climbed forever up through the forest. I had joined it by climbing to it from the cookie lady's house early in the morning. My entrance to it was an old arched stone bridge and a wooden sign that alerted me. The pedal work was difficult as I had not spent an entire day climbing before on my bicycle. The scene unfolded beautifully though in front of my two slowly spinning tires. The road wrapped tightly around the trees and outcroppings of stone switching back and forth as it ascended. After much time had passed I found myself well above the trees and hills below. I stopped at an outlook and met three motorcyclists who were journeying to South America from there to have an adventure of their own that summer. They planned upon returning in the fall and I wished them well as we took photos of each other, the amazing forest canopy as the backdrop. Their bikes were packed with metal saddle bags and camping gear fit for the expedition ahead of them. I hope it served them well.

I took rest breaks when the pedaling got to be to much. I forced myself to pedal every foot of the parkway and stopped all forward progress to rest on the side of the road near the trees. I would later come to walk during such breaks in the day as I became more bent on an always forward mind set. The day was sweaty, hard, and fully rewarding. I had truly accomplished something at the end of it. I mistakenly thought myself finished with the hardest of what the journey probably had to offer in turns of endless climbing. I was just scratching the surface though as I would find out. The day ended with a quick dinner and I slept like a baby.

We started the next day enjoying both hot breakfast and showers. It had been a few days since we had access to such niceties as a shower with heated water and I was happy to clean the boys and myself up. We all had to spend a long time getting clean as we washed days of the road down the shower drain. Then I chased the boys around the bathroom to get them dried off and dressed for the day. On the way back to Isosceles I notice that the camper was dripping water out of the corners and front door. I thought it had rained while we showered just up until Brianne opened the door and it was then that we realized that Isosceles had flooded. Water poured out of the entryway and out onto the gravel around my shower shoes. I was taken aback by the scene unfolding before my eyes. Like a bolt of lightning, Gabriel shot out of the camper and ran off down the road towards the end of the loop we were camped. I gave chase and took the next 15 minutes cornering him between another RV and their truck. When I returned with our crazy 107 pound lab we found that Gabriel had turned on the faucet and not being able to escape the chaos had pooped all over the bed as he must have watched in horror as the camper began to fill with water. I turned off the water pump, which had nothing to pump anymore, and got the jack wrench out of the storage compartment in order to get the camper tilted to one corner. We found out that all you need are a couple of towels and a jack in which to unlevel the trailer to clean up such a debacle. You would never have been able to tell we had a flood and all of the left over moisture dried out over the day. The moment had been very stressful though and added several hours onto my start for the day.

The riding was much tougher than it had been over the past few days as my poor legs were just saturated with lactic acid from the day before riding up the parkway. I tried hard to work through the pain but could not maintain any resemblance of steady pedaling for the entire day. I limped along digging deep into my well of perseverance in order to carry on. It was hard, stressful, and demoralizing. I wanted to hang it all up a couple of times that day and ended my pedaling 16 miles earlier than I had wanted to in the parking lot of a Budget Inn along the route on the edge of Lexington. The ride through Lexington was less pleasant then it should have been as a result of the evening traffic and construction detouring me from the route onto some extreme grades through the back neighborhoods. I had a great deal of trouble meeting up with Brianne and the boys as Lexington was a bigger city than most we stopped in and our use of landmarks to deduce where we were fell short on account of their being so many similar areas around the city.

It was really good to be back with my family when we connected up and things gradually turned better as we drove all around looking for a place to stay. We found a Walmart parking lot but did not feel the area was safe enough for the boys and so we pressed on to a different Walmart in hopes of getting a hot dinner on the stove and a good nights sleep underway before it became too late. The next parking lot was high up on a hill nestled in the mountainous terrain. We parked with the door of the RV facing out from the parking lot to overlook the surrounding mountains. It was a quiet and beautiful place to spend the night. I walked across the vast parking lot and into the store to find a manager in order to let them know we were parked there for the night. A welcoming woman at the customer service counter said, "You are more than welcome to the back of the lot but you need to be on the road by 7:00AM." I thanked her, bought some chocolate and sodas for us back at the camper, and then walked my weary body across the parking lot once more. We had only the 10 volt battery for power that night and did not turn on the propane furnace as it was not too cold when we tucked ourselves in. We covered up with blankets, snuggling together for warmth. The night was frigid later on though and I felt like my skin was on fire as my spent body recovered slumbering in the colder air of the night. I had not felt so completely wiped out in my entire life other than my basic training in the Army at good old fort lost in the woods misery during the summer of 1999. You may know it as Fort Leonard Wood, Missouri though. The total exhaustion was a part of the journey for me though as I have come to know that one can never truly enjoy the warmth of the fire without first experiencing the cold of the night. I embrace this fully.

The morning was rushed as we awoke from the frigid night in the parking lot with about an hour left before we were expected to depart. A heavy fog had settled over the rolling mountain side covering it like a blanket. Brianne made oats for breakfast while I brewed my coffee, too strong. I sipped the bitter concoction as I slowly came back to life. Bitter coffee does a number on my mouth, throat, and digestive system but the extra dose of caffeine feels great! We finished up the dishes and hurriedly packed as we were closing in on this Walmart's 7:00AM exit time. I pulled Isosceles around to a different parking spot facing the exit to show we were fully intending to comply. Then we shopped there to return the favor.

We departed for my starting point back at the Budget Inn parking lot on the edge of Lexington. I made sure to roll up and pack my jacket in my panniers. That was good planning on my part as it did a great job of warding off the rain the day. My ride took my out of the Blue Ridge and into the foothills which then spilled out into a smallish valley full of warm sunshine, colts, and downhill runs. I had my legs back and it felt good to go fast again. The road was spotted with the occasional vulture or three snacking on breakfast, lunch, and I assumed eventually dinner. The road was always full of manna for the scavengers.

My Lunch with Brianne and the boys was very pleasant and then I was off to cruise another 25 miles in what felt like no time at all. I began my ascent later in the day into Christansburg which was very steep, endless, and grueling. The city was most welcoming though and had even posted a sign with a number to call for cyclist services just on the outskirts. I came across it as I was climbing around a switchback on what had to have been a 10 to 12 percent grade. It was another 14 miles to Radford from there and I had planned on going on to another town or two since my legs felt so good but that all changed when I came across a brutal accident on a steep and winding downhill.

I braked carefully as I rode through glass and debris until I came across an SUV buried in a tree on the left side of the road. Another car sat still with its hazards on further down to my right. I looked for the injured to see what could be done to help but found the SUV empty. The occupants of the car were fine.

They were two young men who had just witnessed this horrible accident. They explained that another young man had been driving the SUV at a high rate of speed and rolled it before plowing into the tree. He had broken his arm at the forearm and the female occupant told the witnesses that they did not need nor want their help. A few moments later a van drove up and picked them up leaving the SUV behind. I was a bit taken aback as I could have been in their path had I been there just minutes earlier. I knew that there were risks involved in this adventure and I was willing to take them but it is sad that some people do not consider their actions and what they might do to themselves or others around them.

I called Brianne from an empty lot in Radford and told her I was ready to call it a day at 56 miles after seeing such a horrific accident on my route. We met a friendly couple who owned the lot as we were packing up the bike to head to the RV site down by the river. Brianne and the boys had scoped it out earlier before backtracking for me. The couple told us the history of Rock Road, which we were on, and that it had been used by Daniel Boone to explore the area. Lewis and Clark had an outpost out there too. Daniel Boon, Lewis, and Clark were names that cropped up all along the TransAmerican route. There was also a farm that dated back to the 1700s that people going west would work at in order to afford a ferry ticket to cross the river, explained the gentleman. We thanked our temporary hosts for the use of their lot and the pleasant conversation.

The river side RV park that Brianne and the boys had found was a patch of green space broken up by gravel along the New River. Our site was nestled back against the road and overlooked the river. The sky was overcast and the day was beginning to fade away. I hooked up the water and lifted the hydrant handle to see brown water rush out of our filter and then it slowed to a trickle as it completely clogged the filter. Our six month rated filter was finished in the first state of the journey. I learned from this experience to check the color of the water before passing it through the filter. The rest of the experiences at this park were good as it was quiet and the view was peaceful with the river slowly chugging along. We had lentils in madras curry sauce with sweet peppers and rice for dinner. I then ate half of a box of pasta with taco seasoning. I was still hungry and there were carb burning hills in my future the next day. I was really going to need my legs!

It was another day of climbing endless hills. We had gotten off to a late start too as we packed up camp by the river at around 10:10AM and then drove to the spot where I stopped off the day before in the driveway of the couple we had met. I reassembled my bike, we partially took it apart in order to put it in Isosceles, and we said our goodbyes for the day.

My ride went well at first as I traveled through Radford with ease. I was glad to feel strong in the legs again but it would not last as the hills got the better of me around 35 miles in. We met in Max Meadows, at the top of another big climb. I was so worn out I did not want to eat the lunch provided for me but forced it down anyway. Brianne had parked by the train tracks and the boys' faces lit up as the crossing arms came down and the bells began to clang out. The train blew through town laying hard on its air horn. After lunch I walked over to the small grocery store near the tracks and asked them if they would let me use their restroom. The clerk said there was none but pointed me up the hill to a Lion's club where there were porta potties awaiting me in the hot sun. I was grateful for them though as I sweated inside for a few minutes and headed back to the crossing. We said our goodbyes and I begrudgingly pedaled on but it was hard going.

I could not put anything into the climbs and had nothing in the tank to take advantage of the descents either, which I would normally pedal hard down to help me rise right up the next hill. The wind was steady in my face at 8 mph and it just sucked the joy out of the day. Oh but it gets worse! It started to downpour as I left some lonesome town down the road, which I do not care to remember as it was all hill. The rain was cold and I stopped to put on my jacket and bike lights. It was getting darker out and the lights would be a necessity soon. The path turned onto highway 11 which was kinder because it did not have such steep climbs like the backroads had but it was heavily trafficked and that was no fun in the dim cold rain. I had to start walking up the bigger climbs at this point and had no idea how I was going to make it another 25 miles to Sugar Grove, where we had planned on meeting up for the night. As luck would have it Brianne called me at about 50 miles in and told me it was too rainy for me to push onto Sugar Grove. We would call it a day in Rural Retreat which put me at 55 miles for the day. I was more than happy to agree. Unfortunately for a second time, in-between where I was and where I met my family were some good old boys in a beat up old SUV who thought it would be fun to try to whip me with some type of rubber hose. Lucky for me I always hug the white line to the side of the road as I hear a vehicle approaching from the rear and I did so at this time causing them to miss me. I was lit up inside after that and found the hills and rest of the five miles in the cold rain not such a bother as I wanted to be rid of this place. I was happy to meet up, in one piece thankfully, with my family and I told Brianne about my run in with evil back up the road. We decided we would take a pass on this 18 mile stretch of America and drove on into Troutdale where we stayed at a church hostel for Appalachian Trail hikers and TransAmerican cyclists.

The church pastor met us at the parking lot of the new edition of their church at the bottom of a steep hill. The old church and hostel were up the hill. There was not much chance of us getting Isosceles up there in the mud churned up during the past few days of rain though. The pastor had us stay in the parking lot below and walked me up the hill to show me were the showers and restrooms were. I thanked him for his kindness and smiled at several hikers who were resting on small porches in front of bunk houses. I love seeing other adventuring souls as I feel a kindred with them. We had dinner and nestled in for the night as a gentle mist rained down on us.

We were awoken by the approach of a vehicle that stopped just outside our window. I got dressed and stepped out, stretching my arms to the sky, and went to meet our visitor. It was the pastor's wife and she had gotten up earlier to cook breakfast for all of us travelers staying at the hostel for the evening. The morning was filled with hot grits, coffee, pancakes, new friends and family. I took Aaron up the hill to the bathrooms and we met up with some less weary Appalachian Trail hikers. Aaron was delighted to meet new people and then we walked down the hill, Aaron on my shoulders. I said my goodbyes and started out for the day. Brianne took the boys to church as it was our second Sunday on the road at this point making it a solid week.

On the way out of Troutdale I was greeted on the first turn by a very large and muddy dog who must have found me very interesting as he chased me for half a mile threatening to knock me off my bike if I made a wrong move towards his property. This was my first dog encounter on the route and I was surprised as they were not supposed to start until Kentucky.

I soon found myself in Jefferson National Forest and it was a tranquil work of beauty. The ride was slightly uphill but you would never have noticed because it was along a creek and wound through a little piece of heaven. The air was forest fresh and there were smoldering campfires where horsemen sipped their black coffee from camp mugs kept filled by percolators of old. They looked content as I rode by and they were in no hurry to head out on their rides. I came across the Appalachian Trail at one point and stopped to take a picture of the sign as some hikers walked across the road on their journeys north. A trail angel walked over to us and offered homemade biscuits with ham and gravy. I was so full from my breakfast that I had to decline but can imagine the fresh taste of baking powder biscuits out here in God's great wilderness was to die for. I really needed this serene start to my day after yesterday. The day stayed just as wonderful until I arrived at Hayters Gap.

I ran across another cyclist coming eastbound along the route and we stopped to chat. Steve and two other guys were riding across the country to lay a wreath at the grave of a fallen soldier in Arlington National Cemetery. We spoke of Iraq and exchanged some tips about the trail behind us, his information being of much more value than mine at this point of course. Steve had clued me in on the dogs and trash lined roads ahead of me. His worst dog encounter was with an especially aggressive mutt who had stolen the gloves off his rear bicycle rack. I would later meet what I assume was the same mean spirited K9. As we were talking a small car approached us with some speed and Steve waved downward with his palm to ask them to slow down. A young woman pulled up and asked "Can I help you honey?" Steve replied, "No, I just didn't want to get run over." The young woman smiled at us letting us know she knew why he had waved at her and wished us a good day as she pulled off down the road.

It was good to have run into another veteran along the trail. Steve told me he was ready to be done after the thousands of miles of travel he had endured and we wished each other well as we parted ways. I could not help but wonder what it must feel like to be so near this epic journey's end.

A bit later down the road I skipped the famous Virginia Creeper Trail as I was heading downhill to Damascus. I had heard it was beautiful and shaved a mile off the route but the sweet and well banked downhill turns of the highway begged me to speed on by as fast as my wheels would spin. I am so glad I did too because that extra mile was at 40 mph and so were all of its companion miles to boot. There was no need to brake at every turn because this road was made for cars to fly down at 55 mph. I arrived in Damascus 25 miles from the start of the day in no time flat. It was 10 miles of up through the National Forest and 15 miles almost straight down after that.

I hit the ice cream and fudge shop as I came into town. I parked my bicycle outside of the red and white checkered picnic tables and walked into the shop up a set of wooden stairs. It was a small shop with not much in the way of food choices for vegetarians like myself but it had a cozy feel to it nonetheless. I ordered French fries, grilled cheese, and coffee mixing the kids menu with a caffeinated beverage. What no ice cream or fudge you ask? Not sure what went wrong there but I was happy with the food I did order and I ate it outside in the beautiful sunny day. The town was packed with Appalachian Trail hikers and it was my kind of place. No need to worry about rubber hoses in this part of the country! I was a little sad that I had shaved my winter beard off in May, according to my annual agreement with Brianne that though shall have no beard come May 1, because I was the only guy there without a full one. I spent some time enjoying the food, sun, and passing people before hitting the road again.

I passed a sign that said route 76, the TransAmerican route symbol, left to Yorktown and right to Astoria. I did miss a cool coffee shop somehow though that Brianne told me later that she thought she would find me at when they went through. I really loved Damascus. I was on my way to Meadowview from there where we were to meet for lunch. Yes, another lunch, but I could put away two lunches without even feeling full with all the calories I was burning up into the ether those days.

Brianne and the boys spent some time in Damascus hiking on the Creeper Trail and then caught up with me at a construction site in Meadowview. Lunch was great and I put away half a bag of salt and vinegar chips... Mmm. Conor had to use the restroom so we half opened the camper and set up the porta potty for him. He was so concerned that someone would see him that it took some time for him to finish. Aaron had no problem and went straight to it. After lunch I had about 18 miles left and thought what the heck I could go another 30 for sure! Then came Hayters gap.

Now, I had climbed the Blue Ridge Mountains so what could one three mile mountain summit be to me? This was the most switched back nasty climb I had, until this point, ever made in my entire life. The false summits never ended and I was lost in a purgatory of climbing. Time stopped and the pedaling went on for an eternity. At one point I was completely drenched in salty sweat and the sun made the skin on my back crawl beneath my jersey. You really have not lived until your skin has crawled! After forever had passed came the dark storm clouds and then the accompanying rain. I summited at 3,000 feet above sea level after coming from 1,692 feet below. The climb itself, I think, was over three miles and I wish I could tell you how long it took me but my mind is a bit foggy on that one. I did text some colleagues back in Omaha to joke with them about it though as I needed some comedy relief to restore my sanity. First I rested for a great long moment in the summit parking lot in the steady rain. Then I donned my jacket and zipped it up tight to prepare for the cold rainy descent. Ascents are hot and sweaty almost no matter what the weather and descents are cold and windy. This was not like the descent of the morning as it was switchbacks and wet pavement.

I hit the brakes on the straight aways and leaned in hugging the turns. I made sure not to lean to far in though as the tires might come out from underneath me on the wet road and that would not make for a good end to this glorious day! My right rear brake handle was pressing in further and further into the handlebar as I burned through the brake pad. The front brake began to screech a little as it heated up from the friction created by the constant braking. I was cold and wet! The hills on the other end of the mountain opened up and the terrain was green, rocky, and full of steers.

I came across some cowboys wrestling there cattle into pens, "Hheya hooo hot hot hya!" One cowboy watched on at the fence in dusty denim complete with cowboy hat. It was amazing to see them in action as I passed through their micro world there in rural Virginia. I was close now to the church were Brianne and the boys were waiting for me. It was another hostel for cyclists along the route and in a good spot too as it was between the surrounding towns making it a quiet retreat to rest up before moving on. I had put 57 miles into the day as I pulled up to the church and was greeted by Conor running up to hug me. His excitement to see me every evening touches my soul in a way I suppose only a father could know.

I remember the day the boys were born. It was a chilly misty March morning and I was nervous as we arrived at the hospital parking lot with Brianne who was not worried at all. We checked in and were escorted to a private room where we waited for the surgical team to gather for her C-section. The boys were double breach and there was no chance we were going to go through a natural birth putting her and the boys lives at risk. They took Brianne back first and had me wait outside of the operating room while they prepared her for the operation and waited for the anesthesiologist to arrive. She walked past me and into the room and a few moments later I was invited in. The room spun around a few times as I stood up to enter the place where Aaron and Conor would come into the world. They had me sit down in a chair just off to the left of Brianne's head. She was so excited to see everything that she had them lower the sheet they put up to block the action from the mother as they worked. The following scene that unfolded before my eyes was both horrific and wonderful. They cut quickly suctioning up fluid and blood with a medical grade industrial vacuum. The holding tank was seated on the floor to my right and it filled as the sound of sucking air and fluid reverberated around the room. The bloody liquid began to pool on the floor and run towards my shoes. Brianne watched with what I believe was delight as they delivered first Aaron and brought him to her to see before quickly moving him on to me. One of the technicians asked me about the port wine stains striped across his body and I showed them the matching one on my arm telling her that it was normal for my family for this to occur. He was given an Apgar score of nine and put into a hospital style baby operating bassinet before they cleaned him up. Conor came out next and he was a deep shade of blue. They rushed him by Brianne and I before taking him to have a vacuuming of his airways to clear them of the meconium he had breathed in before birth. He was scored a seven and both were swaddled as they stapled Brianne back together again. The boys were placed with Brianne to be shuttled down the hall to our recovery room. I can still remember the instant bond that I felt for them and the fear I had to hold them in my arms as if they were as fragile as a whiff of smoke that would dissipate should I touch it. They were so light and warm. I put my face to theirs and could smell the new life of them. I still enjoy putting my face to theirs to this day and know soon they will not want such affection from me as they go through childhood on their way to becoming their own independent persons. I also know that they will come back around as they become adults as I have over my life.

I Like to Ride

The kids had been playing on a cool playground full of toys built for the imagination. There were cars and airplanes with mechanisms bringing them to life as the children swayed back and forth in them. To the left was an outdoor shower and a pavilion for cyclists to rest at. Brianne put dinner on in the church kitchen while I watched the boys play. Aaron started walking up the hill behind the church and then raced down it to the pavilion only to repeat this over and over again. I followed him up and was greeted by a lone grave behind a large tree. It was very old and spoke to the length of time this church had been standing there in these rural parts. I took a cold shower outside and it reminded me of the showers I used to take outside at Bagdad International Airport in some wooden quad showers with solar heated water. They were unisex and covered just enough of the body to make them descent for soldiers to shower both male and female side by side in the warmth of the desert sun. There is something so alive, so human, in washing up outside in nature that must be experienced to fully appreciate it. I toweled off my chilled body and went back to the camper to be with everyone. A storm moved in as we bedded down for the night and it was both loud and howling. I was glad to know that I had arrived at the hostel at the right time of the evening to enjoy that time with my family and to clean up before the storm set upon us.

Kentucky

The church we stayed at was located in a great spot as it was close to the border of Kentucky. The day was full of beautiful mountains and ended with the Breaks which was a canyon complete with roaring water and deep treed awe. It was a great site to see. We had our lunch earlier in Haysi, a small town carved out from the surrounding rocks, in front of their library. The shade was welcoming and I put down pickle spears and salt & vinegar chips as fast as my mouth could chew them. Brianne and the boys had made use of the library while I was out riding, playing with the toys and updating the website. It was a small town library with friendly people from the area who suggested we write a book about our travels. I was surprised to learn on the journey that these places were little havens from the sun along the route. They were also one of the best places to find a stable internet connection.

I arrived at the border of Kentucky later in the day with such excitement! I was however under impressed with the sign that announced the change. It was a small lone sign and I shared a moment of time with it. Perhaps it was fitting as my journey had really just begun with thousands of miles of road laying ahead of me on my way to the other coast. The border between the two states was mountainous and I guess I had not thought about all of the climbing I would be doing in the first part of the journey because I felt less prepared for it than I should or could have been. At some point on one of the many ascents that week I had hurt my left knee. I think I had been overusing both of them in those mountains as they were accustomed to the plains of Nebraska and Iowa.

The rest of the day was a bit of a drag with the knee injury and I did not know what to think of the Eastern edge of Kentucky as it was riddled with trash along the roadsides. It felt like stepping into another world and reminded me of some parts of war torn Iraq in 2004. There were a few used hypodermic needles and prescription bottles strewn about as well. All of the people I ran into had been very friendly though and this helped to make up for the riding conditions.

The homes were dotted along beautiful mountain streams that seemed to run endlessly in, out, over, and under the homes, roads, and rocks. One thing for sure is that these people know how to garden. I had learned so much from them just by passing through and I was excited to use their techniques in our home garden once the growing season was upon us again the next spring.

Brianne saved me about 15 miles from our stopping point for the day and that was truly a blessing as I was walking up the steep inclines now, unable to put to much torque on my injured knee. I rested it and sucked down three Advil along with a Coke to ward off any impending swelling. I was worried about the ride the next day as we had to be in Mammoth Cave by the following Saturday in order to hold the family gathering Brianne had planned for the families of children with Ohtahara Syndrome.

Our son Aaron was diagnosed with this early onset epilepsy and we started a nonprofit focused on promoting awareness, research, and support like this gathering. We have been honored over the years to be able to meet up with such fine people and their beautiful children. We really enjoy it and keep the flame of hope alive in our hearts that more will be known and done for this syndrome in the future. The first couple of months of Aaron's life were a rollercoaster of such pain and anguish. We had noticed a peculiar difference between him and his sibling Conor within a few hours after their births. Aaron was attempting to sit up through his tightly wrapped swaddle and Conor was not anywhere near such an advanced movement. It took us all day to convince someone that something was amiss with Aaron. We were treated like the new parents that we were, as if we had no idea what we were talking about. When Aaron stopped breathing they took his condition a bit more seriously.

We arrived at the Baptist church where we planned on spending the night. There was an old playground where the paint had long pulled away from the metal equipment. You could hear the creek running behind the building but could not see it through the dense brush on either side. The children played on the playground while Brianne prepared dinner in the camper. We were grateful for the refuge and a little nervous being so far removed from the urban areas we had grown accustomed to over the years. The night came quickly deep in the draw of the mountain in Lookout, Kentucky. We slept well.

We met Alice, our gracious host, at the Baptist Church Community Center when we woke up. She let us into the center and we got to talk with everyone who was there to provide much needed support for this local community. They run a clothing and food distribution center for families in the area. I was so impressed by their generosity as they were handing out everything from clothing to vitamins. They had me sign the cyclist ledger and I saw that Micheal had been there two nights before me. I knew we would not cross paths again as he was a stronger rider than I but was glad we got the chance to meet. I hope his journey was swift with the wind always at his back. He had wanted to be done in 71 days and would have no trouble accomplishing his goal.

I started to think my 90 day estimate was a little crazy as I was starting day 11 right on schedule but with a knee injury not readily healing itself. I had settled on 90 days because of the sabbatical outlined in the employee handbook from my previous job. We planned the trip using the Adventure Cycling maps and Google Maps from there.

The mountains were beginning to get a little nicer as we were getting closer to the end of their range. They had been something out of this world for me and I had to swallow my pride on numerous occasions hopping off the saddle and favoring my right leg to walk up a few of the sharper grades to save my knee. My riding sandals clicked and made grinding sounds as their cleats met the road. The day had started out good. We deployed pepper spray to the handlebar bag after heading the advice from the women at the church. They had warned us of the dogs on the other side of the mountain. I especially picked up on one recollection of another man who had come from the other way and stayed the night there. He had used an alpha voice with the dogs and told them how good they were as if he were their owner. I have to tell you that he was right on the money. I was attacked by six sets, yes sets, of dogs during the course of the day and it worked on every last one of them. No bites for me and I still had a full can of pepper spray!

Well, the day had two good sized mountains but was mostly a gradual up and down. I was baked under the harsh sun on one mountain top and got to experience the cool of the evening as I pushed on further than I thought I would have been able to with my knee pain. At one point I sat under the shade of a post office awning watching the sun begin to set over the ridge line of the trees. I had liked Kentucky so far. It was not as clean as

Virginia but it felt less worried about the little things and maybe a bit forgotten.

Brianne iced down my screaming knee when I got into Dwarf, Kentucky after a 67.8 mile day. It felt so good to rest it finally. I hoped it would not prematurely end my ride or cause me to have to take a few days off before our gathering. I would do what I could and leave it all on the road either way just like coach O used to tell us in high school football right before a Friday night game. "Leave it all on the field!" We had mac and cheese for dinner accompanied by salty olives and a sweet Coke. I was so tired and just ready to sack out for the evening. That night I dreamt of mountains.

The morning started off a bit earlier than the last few days. I wanted to get a move on the day to beat the heat. I packed up Isosceles and helped Brianne get things ready to go for the day before I set out. The first part of the morning was a steep climb but it went well in the cool air. I found a McDonalds six miles in and stopped for some coffee and an egg with cheese biscuit. The news was on and they were talking about the Democratic party's primary. I was glad to be out of the political news cycle for a change and the stress it can bring. Both sides like to whip up a sense of doom if their opponent wins. They must know that people tend to run off their fears sometimes.

I rolled out of there as fast as I had come and turned off down the next county road. It went instantly upward, they all seemed to around Kentucky, and I was attacked by several dogs. I used my technique from the day before and it worked on every aggressive dog except for one. I knew this was the dog Steve had warned me about in Virginia because he was especially vicious. I saw one large dog along the path on an up-hill climb and girded myself for his attack but he cowered off down the mountain side to my right. I thought to myself that this was strange but then a middle sized demon came barreling out of the forest to my left and made a line straight for me. I pedaled hard, telling him what a good dog he was in my deep-est voice, as he was trying his damnedest to bite into my calves. His snarls filled the air around me as I was standing on the pedals now swinging back and forth with momentous effort to escape. In the end I was saved by my two rear panniers which he sunk his teeth into as a consolation for missing my legs. I could hear the anger in him from behind me as I tried desper-ately to dig for my pepper spray in the right pocket of the han-dlebar bag. Damn if it was not buried beneath a granola bar and a tangerine. The drawstring that held them there also barred my prying fingers. I abandoned the spray. I had to focus on pedaling as he tore holes in each pannier ripping and gnash-ing with his foaming snarl of a mouth. I finally out pedaled him after about a quarter mile. My heart was jacked up on adren-aline and it was a good long while before it found a normal ca-dence again. He was by far the most aggressive dog that I have ever run into on any bicycle ride. Later I heard of a man who had gone through the same area a few days before me and had gotten bitten by what I can only assume was this dog. He had to go to the hospital to get his leg stitched back together ending his epic journey on those back mountain roads. This attack made it nine groups of dogs now for me and Brianne reported six having gone after her while she was driving. There are plen-ty of warnings from other cyclists about the dogs in Kentucky. No exaggeration is needed as these dogs do love a good chase.

Soon I was in the heat of the day and began to run out of water. The steep climbs caused me to walk many miles as my knee would not allow for repetition up grades anymore. The air was still and humid with a hot sun just getting started for the approaching summer. I ran out of water twice throughout the day and decided to bring another 32 ounce bottle with me starting the next day. I would also get up at 5:30AM to make sure I was on the road well before the heat could turn me into the burnt out mess of a person I had become that day. By the time I had made it into the last town, Boonville, I was parched and stopped at a local grocery store. I parked my bicycle outside by the soda machine and dragged myself into the cool sweet air conditioning. I wandered around the florescent lighted isles in search of cold soda and ice cream. When I made it over to the checkout lane the lady behind the counter treated me like a homeless wanderer. I was a bit taken aback and offended at first but then found this humbling experience that was offered to me to be a gift which would soften my heart later as I came across others in such a shape.

Brianne had found a local church that we could stay at and they had a shower! It was super cold, good for my burnt out husk of a body, but a challenge for us with the boys as we had to chase them around to get them into it. Aaron cried and screamed as I bathed him as quickly as possible. Conor was less than thrilled too but we all ended up fresh again. Brianne planned on doing our laundry at the local laundry mat in the morning after I got underway. We needed a laundry run at this point.

While Brianne cooked supper a man was dropped off at the church. He was riding in the back of a white pickup truck and hopped out walking up to the drivers window to thank them before they rolled off. He walked over to the far end of the back lot of the church and sat down under the wind shelter they had set up for cyclists. Brianne urged me to introduce us to the gentleman and I went out to strike up a conversation with him while she finished setting the food out onto plates. He was from Scotland, here for a year to wander America without aim. He told me about the places he had been and that he could stare at the Rocky Mountains for days on end as they were just so beautiful. That he really like the people who lived in Montana most of all and that their motels were the most reasonably priced. He also suggested I make my way up to the Dakotas as they were flatter and would make for easier pedaling. I did not ask his name and nor did he offer it. The sky began to sprinkle on us as we spoke and I helped him assemble his tent before the worst of the rain began to pour down out of the humid evening sky. I jogged back to our camper wishing him well on the end of his journey before I left. He was gone before we arose the next morning and I hoped his travels were safe and full of adventure.

The morning started early as Aaron was raring to go. I was glad to get a move on too, to try and skip the heat of the day saving myself a repeat of the day before. Well, boy was I surprised when it started down pouring 15 minutes into the ride and never let up. I turned off the main road and down another backwoods road passing by logging operations where the crews were packing up to escape the rain. I turned the lights on my bicycle to strobe in order to allow them a better chance of seeing me as they drove their trucks by in the low visibility. The water was coming down the road, which had become a stream, and the turnouts were a wash out of mud slowing my progress up the hills. I was completely soaked but I had become familiar with this condition so it bothered me less than it had before.

Eventually, I came across a gas station located across from a school on another main road. I imagine the Adventure Cycling route made use of these side roads to keep us cyclists out of traffic and as deep into nature as possible. The path is beautiful. I parked my bike on the sidewalk near a set of plastic lawn chairs and an outdoor table. The rain from the roof dripped over my head as I walked to the door and went inside. There were a few older gentleman drinking coffee at a table in the center of the store. I walked past them and took a Styrofoam coffee cup from a slip on the back table. The coffee was in an old style glass container sitting on a warming plate and I poured the black crude into the cup. I found the artificial cream and real sugar off to the side and stirred them in with a plastic stir straw. These straws always remind me of my grandparents bar in Rolla North Dakota. I used to sip my soda through them in those old style small beer glasses. I walked past the men and up to the counter to pay for the drink. The young woman be-hind the counter gave me the hobo in the rain look as she took my money. I must have looked kinda crazy sopping wet in my riding jersey and shorts. I trudged outside with my warm cof-fee and sat down in a lawn chair, the sides bending against my weight. The coffee warmed my hands and my throat giving me a peaceful moment out of the rain under the overhang. I was about 21 miles into the day and had 11 more to go before reach-ing our lunch destination. Brianne and the boys were most like-ly still at the laundry mat in Boonville and I imagined it would take them some time to catch up with me. Finally, a day where I was waiting on them instead of the other way around!

I recalled the baby turtle I had stopped to save in the road earlier. I had missed the opportunity to save a grown one as a truck came barreling down the road at the same moment that I was dismounting to pick it up. The truck went right for the turtle and there was nothing I could do. I knew why there were so many dead turtles in the road in these parts as it appeared to be open season on them. There was less trash on the side of the road in this part of Kentucky and I was only chased by two dogs so far.

As I starred off past the gas pumps and into the rainy day a gentleman left the store and walked over to me. He opened a pack of unfiltered cigarettes, fetched from his front shirt pocket, and lit one. He told me that he used to own this gas station and knew that I was riding cross country as he had seen many cyclists come through over the years. He enjoyed riding his motorcycle all over and had ridden it across America too. We related to each other with some of our similar experiences. He did not have the same trouble with the dogs as I had around these parts but he was moving faster than they could run. I told him that my grandfather smoked unfiltered cigarettes all of his life up until they killed him. He had lived a long life though and we cannot live forever. I miss the smoked turkeys he used to make when we came up North to visit him and my grandmother. They owned a hotel that was attached to their bar. My grandfather would hunt game and my grandmother cooked it for us. The duck would always have those little lead balls of shot in them that you would have to watch out for as you ate. She was a great cook and I always found visiting them to be an adventure. We said goodbye and I hopped on my saddle to ride off towards lunch.

I ended up being late for lunch, again, by about 20 minutes as the laundry mat Brianne waited at never opened their doors and I had dallied at the gas station for a good hour. I was chased down by some more dogs on the way putting the total around 11 now for the trip. One pair was so fast that I could not outrun them at 22 miles per hour! One of them got out in front of me while the other chased from behind. How peaceful it would be to be rid of the unleashed and free range dogs as I left the state in a week or so... I met up with Brianne and the boys as I entered Berea. We headed off to a laundry mat to do our wash. The laundry mat was a little run down but it did the trick. We got into a conversation with a woman there who entertained Conor with his silly talk for a while. I accidentally left my map of the Appalachian Mountains there as it must have fallen out of my back pocket while I was chasing the kids around. It was sad to have lost it as it had been a steady companion but Berea was the end of that map and I would not need it anymore. We did go back to look around for it but someone else must be on their very own adventure up in those mountains being entertained by the wild aggressive dogs! After our clothes were clean we went to get the oil changed since we had gone far enough for the SUV to warn us it was time. We dropped Isosceles off at an RV campground first though to make it easier. I waited in the parking lot with Gabriel as Brianne went shopping inside with the boys. We were in and out in under an hour. Walmart had done a quick and great job. The technician alerted me to a burnt out bulb in the rear of the vehicle and I bought one off the shelf for around a dollar. They are easy to replace and cost almost nothing if you do the work yourself. After shopping we headed over to a place to have a pizza for dinner. It was a local place and the pizza was good.

Back at the RV site it was certainly a treat to have full hookups and a little patch to call home for an evening. The fresh water tank was full again and I spent the next couple of hours building the new bicycle wheel to replace the other rear wheel when I had run out of spokes for it. I had it all laced up but not tightened and trued yet. It began to rain a little again as we drifted off to sleep. The sound of the drops tapping on the roof of the camper were soothing. The next couple of days promised to be wet, then hot, and ultimately muggy. The good news though was that I was on map 10 now and the changes in elevation would be measured by every 200 feet instead of 1,000 as they were on map 11. There were more hills to come of course but nothing like the never ending ones in the Appalachian Mountains. I had conquered those.

The next day was really hot and I was beginning to get a picture of how the climate was going to progress until I was able to cycle myself up into the higher elevations of the Rocky Mountains. That would be in several weeks though and there I was in the flatter parts of Kentucky pedaling onward. I ended up taking a different route out of Berea and into the rural backroads where the trail picked back up. I rode through light morning traffic in a couple of neighborhoods and then had to stop for a spell to figure out which direction I was supposed to be heading. I got underway down the real route at a great pace while the sun started to rise to my right warming my cheek. The road was mostly flat with some hills and there must have been a bit of a breeze behind me because I was hitting 20 miles per hour for a good stretch of it. I turned down another road next to a barn with a sign on it warning of a reward for farm thieves courtesy of some organization I cannot recall and the pace slowed from there as my breeze was now slightly cross with me. I eventually exited that road near a shop that only the locals and occasional random cyclist would have known even existed. The shelves were sparse but held snack cakes and there was a cold soda for me as well. I passed a couple of ranchers on the way out the door and sat against a wooden fence to enjoy my carb and fat filled fuel. One of the ranchers walked over to me as he was leaving and struck up a conversation. It turned out that this rancher had built a shelter for cyclists out on his ranch right before Harrisburg. I thanked him for his kindness and walked back in to see if I could fill my water bottles as I had found it best to keep them full at this point. The woman who owned the store beamed with pride as she told me, "I fill all of the cyclists bottles as they pass through these parts." I was glad to have been one of them moreover to have been able to help support her business even if it was just the small price of snack cakes and soda. I took off down the road which took me by a lake with a marina and restaurant. I had wanted to stop in for a bite to eat but had neither the time nor the extra spending money. The place was beautiful though and I enjoyed passing through. It reminded me of an episode of some house hunting show Brianne and I had watched a couple of months before where they were buying homes on a lake to live in. There were such homes here too. After crossing the bridge and heading up a hill around a bend I came across a tree and sought shelter from the sun. I was not doing so well with the heat of the day upon me and those shade breaks were necessary as the sun got really going in the early afternoon. I found a strange moth crossing the road while I rested. It was very large, brown, and walked with its wings dragging across the road sideways. It was a new species for me and I watched it awhile before moving on. A couple of miles down the road there was a bad accident between a garbage truck and an SUV. I dismounted from the bike and walked through the scene exiting the other side. There were long lines of traffic, sherifs, and an ambulance. A guy called out from his truck in the long line of vehicles to tell me I was the lucky one as I did not have to wait there with the rest of them to get on my way. I thought to myself that he was the lucky one sitting in the air conditioning as the hot sun intensified with the lack of wind created by the movement of the bike. I guess we were both lucky compared to the occupants of the SUV.

The rest of the day was hot and sunny with a small breeze that seemed to be in my face on the uphills. It had pushed me up a few big ones though so I should not be too harsh in my remembrance of it. Later in the day I stopped at the front of a large property with a winding road leading up to a church. I rested under a shade tree. It was only four more miles to meet up with Brianne and the boys but I was so hot and badly needed the rest. I drank a great deal of water and then pushed on the last four miles.

I took a wrong turn once I got into town and passed out of it going the wrong direction. This rarely happened anymore now that I really had only one way to go or turn for the most part but this town was a bit larger than the others I had been passing through. I stopped and got out Google Maps on my phone to see where I had gone wrong. I turned around and headed back up a hill to a gas station at the turn I was supposed to take. It was time for a break after that nonsense and so I stopped in. The women running the counter were kind enough to cook me an egg and cheese biscuit and I sipped coffee outside while enjoying the hot meal. A small beagle shimmied up to me and tried to drink my coffee. He looked tired and dirty as if he had been living outside for a bit. A woman opened up the door and went in with him following, unbeknownst to her. He was later escorted back out to sit with me. One of the clerks got a number from his collar and called a disconnected line. I would have been happy to take him down the road with me but I had no way of safely doing so and everyone there seemed to know who he belonged to but had no idea how to contact them. They settled on the animal clinic in the next county over and that was that. I bid my little snack companion safe travels and took off to find Brianne and the boys. I was able to catch them on my cell phone and arranged to meet them down the road a couple of more towns as I had felt refreshed from the pit stop. The heat proved too much for me though as I had to throw in the towel around Rose Hill about 58 miles into the day. This was the next town over and I felt a little defeated by loosing my stamina so easily in-between the two. I sat on a bench outside a convenience store there sipping an orange soda while I waited for Brianne to come swoop me up for the night. When she arrived we broke the bike down and put it in the camper. From there we drove to the home of president Abraham Lincoln's parents and spent the night in the parking lot by the pavilion. It was a bit difficult to find but not too far from where we called it a day. We had arrived right before the gift shop had closed. The man running the place let us know that they put up cyclists there, that they had bathrooms, and a place to charge our phones. We set up Isosceles and then walked through the exhibits learning about Lincoln's family. His mother had fallen ill after drinking milk tainted by a weed that the cow had eaten and died from her illness. It was a little scary to think that would be a possible ending for us if we had less control over what our cows were eating. The night was no cooler than the day and the kids and I passed out from the heat around 10PM. When it got really dark the fire flies came out in numbers. They lit up the night like summer evenings spent as a child long ago. There was also a brilliant thunder storm off in the distance that tried to compete with them but I can say without a doubt that they out performed the storm.

I started the morning right as the sun was rising over the fields adjacent to the parking lot where we had spent the night. I got out my phone and looked at Google Maps to get my bearings. It was difficult to tell from the map which way I should be heading as there was no data service and because of this the map would not fill in the pertinent information I needed to make such a decision. The sun helped by letting me know which way was west but the TransAmerican Road sign down the road pointed me in a direction that made no sense. I rode down about a mile in the way the sign pointed me but began to get the feeling I was off track and so I stopped to speak with a gentleman mowing the golf course that was off to my right. He kindly let me know why I was so turned around. Apparently Kentucky changed the traditional route to create a tourism opportunity. Once I had this information I could safely ignore the route signs and head in the direction he pointed out as being the old way people used to travel. I was back on track within 30 minutes and it felt great to know where I was going.

I Like to Ride

I started churning out the miles as the wind is apt to sleep in, giving me a vacuum to move in, and the sun stayed hidden behind some clouds keeping the temperature just right for pushing oneself. I made it a good 22 miles before I stopped at a gas station for a packaged cheese Danish and a cup of coffee. People still steered clear of me as I looked a bit like a wanderer still and this suited me just fine as I enjoyed the solitude those days afforded me. I had chosen to grow out my beard as it was easier to maintain on the road and I used my homemade beard oil to keep it fresh and soft. Brianne and I had started a side business selling home made soaps, chapstick, and beard oil the previous fall for some fun. We had sold our wares at craft fairs and had made a small profit so far as the initial investment was small and the margins really good even at a low asking price.

I had created the beard oil blend the winter before to soften my winter riding beard as it had become dry and scratchy. I had challenged myself to ride around the lake near our home in the coldest weather possible. I would get up around 4AM and layer myself in flexible warm clothing before heading out into the ever increasingly intense elements. There were joggers down by the lake who layered as well and we all looked like we were wearing high tech wet suits by January. My new goal by then was to ride out there one morning on a day they had deemed too cold to jog on. It was a tough challenge as they were just as crazy as I was. When the wind chill reached negative 30 degrees though I could not shift my rear gears as the derailleur was too cold to move on its own. I had to stop and adjust it with my hands to find a good single gear to stick with. The joggers had stayed home that day and I declared victory.

There I was at a gas station in Kentucky warding people off with my unkempt style! I was getting to know the people who knew what I was up to at this point in the journey across America as they seemed to seek me out where others were shunning me now. They were always curious as to where I was coming from and to where I was headed. Some would recall speaking with other cyclists over the years and many were fellow travelers of a sort or wished to be on the road like I was.

The rest of the day took me through farmland and up and down some hills. I was able to reach Brianne on the cell phone and let her know where I would be stopping for the day. I came upon a church as I entered a small town and their entrance was a welcome shelter from the sun, which had come out of hiding and was heating the air up rapidly. I settled in and drank water from my bottle. Just then a motorcycle passed me while I rested there under the arched doorway. He flew by on his chrome ride and about one minute later came back from where he had gone parking behind my bicycle. He had the look of a traveler too. He slowly removed his helmet and placed it on his bike seat before turning to slowly walk up to where I rested. He introduced himself to me but you will have to forgive me throughout my recounting of people I had met along the trail because I am a face person and seldom remember a name. I always remember the background and the image of the person though like a video I can replay over and over recalled by the electrical impulses of my mind. We spoke of the long trail ahead and he let me know he had been putting people up for years in his home down the way. "The last guy was from China" he exclaimed! "The first Communist that had ever stayed in my home." He was a cool guy and you could tell he liked talking to people about where they have been and where they were headed. The gentleman from China was passing through from the West to the East in December and it was getting cold out at night. I cannot imagine the weather got much friendlier as he got into the Appalachian Mountains of Eastern Kentucky.

The gentleman went on his way motoring off down the road. Brianne arrived about 10 minutes later and picked me up. I was glad for it as the sun had really come out now and that was my witching time! Forty-eight miles down for the day but many more to go in the journey. I was getting closer to 1,000 miles though! We planned on celebrating with some sparkling grape juice we had brought from home. The boys could join in with that. I also had some 18 year old Scotch. This was the end of the forced pedaling as it was time to head south to the family gathering Brianne had planned.

We drove down the Mammoth Cave loop to meet up with some of the families who had come for the Aaron's Ohtahara Foundation family gathering. They were staying at an RV park with a playground and all sorts of fun stuff for the kids to get up to. We enjoyed some frosty brews and good company as we all caught up on what our families were up to over the past year. I attempted to fix a leak in the water line of one of the campers at the site but could not find it for the life of me. It was buried inside the sidewall behind the cabinets where it leaked out onto the ground but not inside of the camper. The boys played with the other children and we relaxed for a few hours. From there we headed to the Hampton Inn to meet up with another family who Conor had made close friends with their daughter the year before in Boston. We stopped by Pizza Hut to pick up some pizzas and then promptly got lost following the

GPS on the way to their hotel. The GPS took us deep into the surrounding forest on what I could only assume was its idea of the shortest route. The road narrowed to one lane and we traveled on for a long while before finding a dirt road to back Isosceles into to turn around. We eventually got to the hotel and enjoyed semi-warm stuffed crust pizza and more good company. The boys and I went for a swim and then it was time for a hot tub which eased away the pain in my overworked muscles. The night concluded with me doing some minor wood repair work on Isosceles in the truck stop across from the hotel. The bench bed had broken at the ledge the day before. We had the good fortune of having the proper tools on hand to fix it and I went to work creating new pilot holes for the screws. It took about an hour to make it right again but was well worth the effort as we were back to two beds now.

We boondocked there at the truck stop in-between two other RV's. A man exited the one in front of us and assembled a large round metal cage before producing 12 small Pomeranian dogs. I assumed this was how he rounded up their poop in order to make cleaning up after them possible. They yipped about for 30 minutes and then back into the RV they went for the night! When we awoke the next day I guessed we might have overstayed our welcome by about an hour as we noticed the other RV's were out in a hurry by 7AM and we were getting out around 8AM. As we were finishing up with the pack-up a sheriff drove up and parked next to us. Either he was there for something else entirely or he saw we were almost all set to take off because he did not get out to speak with us. I decided to make it a point to be on the road by 7AM next time we boondocked though as that seems to be the right time and was the time the last Walmart we stayed at gave us too.

Mammoth Cave day! I only biked a mile that day and with no panniers on. I will never forget the difference between my bike loaded with gear and how agile it felt empty. It really glides when I am the only weight on it. My morning rides back in Omaha were going to be fast as lighting when I returned! We fueled up the SUV with gasoline and me with coffee at the truck stop on the way out to the cave. The cave was not far away and the day was a rest day which I was literally in sore need of. The coffee was good, I got a medium size instead of the small I usually have to get to keep on schedule and after yesterday the only hard date we really needed to hit was the kids first day of school in the second week of August.

We arrived at the park entrance and took a family photo outside of the sign. We then moved into the park and there were tons of parking spots for regular cars and RV's alike. We spent the next hour trying to get the keys to our shelter, make accommodations for Gabriel, and find everything. The dog hotel turned out to be an outdoor affair and we decided he would spend the day with us. After we backed Isosceles into a great spot just outside of our shelter the parking lot filled in to capacity right before our eyes. We found out later that over 40,000 people had been there that day! People from all over the world were there and we knew why once we were in the cave.

This cave system lived up to its mammoth name. The head of the park and the public relations manager took us on the first ride on their new elevator. This made the cave accessible for the children with us who were in wheelchairs. The ride was 270 feet straight down. It was cold and dark down there! We walked through the cave admiring the crystalline ceiling that only forms in dry cave systems. There were names written in black lamp soot from the 1800s in one of the caverns. I had thought they were graffiti from recent times at first until our guides told us the stories behind most of them. I was unaware that some of the first cave guides there had been slaves. At another point they shut off the lights and we experienced total darkness. I carried Aaron on my shoulders and held Conor's hand while Brianne trekked on out on point. The rangers showed us a point in the cave where certain octaves of humming caused a vibration in the cave walls. They asked for a volunteer to keep a certain pitch which I was eager to do. My humming washed back over me and around me for some time after I had stopped. It was a really neat experience. Aaron leaned into my cheek from above and was delighted by the sound. He hummed along a little with me too! On the way out of the cave we encountered some cave crickets! These things looked a bit like spiders. I was glad to be on the surface after the long ride up the elevator. It was hot out but it felt good to be out under the wide open sky again. What a great day.

It was fun to spend time with everyone and to see people we had not seen in years. We even got to meet a new mother and her child. The boys had a great day too. After the festivities were concluded and we had cleaned up, everyone pitched in and made light work of it, we were off to our family's rest days at a nearby lake. Brianne had reserved three nights there about eight months before our trip and it was a perfect place to relax. We even got to ride a ferry across a river which ran through the path of the road. The sign on the way down to the ferry read

"Road ends in water." How fitting for such a journey that ended in the Pacific Ocean. It was getting later and the sun was starting to recede as we drove through the forest to our camp site in Nolin State Park. We had full hook ups which meant comfort day and night. The camp site was a level gravel pad with a bench and fire pit. There were showers right down the road and it was a little piece of heaven.

Brianne dropped me off on the route where we had left off after we spent three days in Mammoth cave exploring and resting. My knee felt ten times better and I was eager to see how it would perform now that I had let it heal. It did not whine at all and I was so grateful for that. The day was uneventful as I pedaled on to our destination in a small town that Brianne had called ahead to get permission to stay in their park. When I arrived I found the children playing on a large playground with some local kids. Brianne was on the swings and I joined her. The park was really large and had an old stadium in it that must have served as a venue for multiple local sports and entertainment at one time. There was a shower and flush toilets along with RV hookups too. I helped Brianne park in the field near a shade tree and we deployed Isosceles. There was a man staying in an RV next to the shower house who had been there for some time. He had been permanently injured while working and now lived there alone. He showed us around the shower house and then returned to watching movies in his RV. Conor kept trying to peak in the open door every time we walked past but I told him he was being impolite. Later in the evening a woman rode up to the pavilion across the field by the playground. We met her as we were walking back with the children to get one last round of fun in before dinner. Her name was Katie and she had been riding with Amy, who we had met on the first night. Amy had stayed in Berea to meet up with her family and Katie had trekked onward. We let her get settled in as we played in the setting sun. Brianne came over when dinner was ready and introduced herself to Katie too. We let her know she was welcome to eat with us whenever she wanted to along the trail and we headed back across the stadium and the field to eat. After dinner two more riders rode into the park and came over to our area. Brianna and Noah were their names and they were riding across most of America having started in upstate New York. They were planning on finishing in Colorado Springs where they had family. We gave them the same tour that the other gentleman had given us before we showered and went to bed.

The next day started off early in the Fordsville park. I helped Brianne with prepping Isosceles for an easy exit when her and the boys were ready to hit the road. I was the first rider on the trail that morning. Katie looked like she was going to be ready to leave about ten minutes after me as I rode by the pavilion and then the playground on the way out of the park. Brianna and Noah had not stirred from their tents yet and it was just me and the open road again. The day went by fast as it started out with only a few climbs but then quickly melted into flat wide open road through vast green and brown fields. I put 25 miles away before stopping to refill my water and then 46 more before stopping again. I did pop my eighth spoke just as I was headed into Sebree, the ending town for the day. I stopped to make sure the wheel was true enough to finish the next mile and then rode on into town. Brianne flagged me down from the porch outside of the house across from the church where we planned to stay at. She was having tea with Violet who was the retired pastor's wife. Violet gave me a towel to dry off from the light rain I had just rode through and a warm cup of coffee. The boys were at play with her grandchildren's toys and her sister was chasing them around the house. I have never felt so welcomed by a complete stranger in my entire life. She opened up the church to us and we had hot showers, laundry, a kitchen, games, and the internet. It had been one of our best overnights yet. Remember to stop at the First Baptist church in Sebree, Kentucky should you ever embark on the TransAmerican Trail. Katie arrived shortly after and met with Violet too as we settled in at the church. We backed Isosceles into a stall and hooked up the power. Gabriel stayed in the camper with the air conditioning as Violet had instructed us to keep him out of the church where there was a congregant who was deathly allergic to dogs. Brianna and Noah arrived a couple of hours later and we all got to spend some more time getting to know each other. We were all invited to dinner with Violet and her husband, Bob, in the evening and it was a real treat. Violet had gone all out to provide a feast for us all in her home. Bob entertained Aaron with their cuckoo clock and after he was sufficiently worn out Noah took over. Aaron just had a ball with that clock. It was an Amish made wooden clock that sang different songs as it did its mechanical act. Throughout the meal Bob listened intently to all of our stories.

After dinner there was homemade lemon pie and ice cream. Violet showed us her scrapbook of all the riders who had been through there and corresponded with her over the last 30 years. It felt like a family gathering and we were truly blessed to be there. Bob prayed for our safe journeys, offering a blessing to each and every one of us in a personal way.

I headed out early again the next morning. The route was filled with wide open flat farmland making pedaling an afterthought. I killed 21 miles and stopped for coffee at my new favorite breakfast place in Kentucky. It was egg and cheese biscuit time with a side of caffeine and cream! The coffee was surprisingly great at Jeri's in Clay, Kentucky, as it should have been on account that Violet had recommended we stop there along the way. Katie pulled up as I was finishing my fourth cup and I recommended she try out the place too. She asked me to watch her bike as she went in and I did so while enjoying the light bustle of the little town before my eyes. When she was all ordered up I wished her a safe and happy ride. I was off again. The route took me right off the main road and onto a side country road that passed the last few homes in town before spilling back out into the countryside. I rode another 30 miles before meeting up with Brianne and the boys in Marion. We were very close to the border of Illinois now and I was excited to cross on the ferry that I had seen in a documentary about the race that took place on the route the year before. The lead racers had been heading east and the ferry was about the end of the line for them as they were traveling almost nonstop, covering hundreds of miles without rest each day. I had just reached the same ferry but heading west. It had taken me about the same amount of time to get there as it did for them to cross the entire country.

From Marion we headed into Amish country and stopped at Yoder's Variety, a general store. I love those kinds of country stores as they are chock-full of good things to eat! It reminded me of the store I stopped in at during my ride across Iowa a couple of years before. There were fresh baked pies and dry goods to enjoy. I had asked the young bearded man behind the counter how they kept the rabbits from eating their gardens up as the one outside of the store was pristine and had no fence around it. He looked at me like anyone should know the answer to that and laughed a bit. He never did tell me how but I imagine it was because they were always looking after it. We purchased some fresh cheese, soap, and candy at Yoder. Katie rode up and stopped in the parking lot to chat with us as we ate before heading on ahead to cross the Ohio River. I enjoyed the cheese thoroughly with our tortillas, they keep great on the road, and then followed suit about 20 minutes later.

The ferry across the Ohio River was just about six more miles down the road and I was really excited to put another state under my tires. I was digging in my rear panniers reaching far behind me while riding down the road when a voice called from my left, "Now that takes talent!" I looked over and saw a fellow rider rocking some tunes and enjoying life. He slowed down and kept pace with me so we could talk along the way to the line for the ferry. He told me he was an Adventure Cycling tour guide and that he was doing the sweep work for the day. He and his counterpart traded days riding in the support vehicle and then making sure no one was in trouble by riding in the rear for the entire day. He was on his third attempt to cross the country, having been stopped by car accidents the other two times. I had known that this was a possibility out on the open road but it hit home a little more to hear him recount the incidents and how they had put an end to his epic journey far too early both times. He was riding with a new counterpart as the other one had been hit by a car the week before. One of his riders was also severely injured when a dog bit his leg in the Appalachian Mountains and I knew just which dog it had to have been. We spoke of positive things too, such as how I could become a tour guide for Adventure Cycling. He explained the process which involved a class at one of several locations where you learn how to be a safe and resourceful touring cyclist. From there you need basic life saving skills such as CPR and first aid. I was thinking check and check! I had learned all sorts of skills in the military and would just need to get certified again. Heck I have even been known to put in an IV or two in a war zone but trust me when I tell you there are much better people at it such as my wife Brianne who was a paramedic in Kansas City before we were married. The leadership course he spoke of was something I was interested in doing but I needed to find out how or if it would fit into my life plans upon returning to Nebraska after this glorious adventure. We waited in the ferry line behind Brianne and the boys. Brianne got out of the SUV and took our picture before the line moved on and up the ramp off the ferry. We rode near the guard rails beside the cars. The ride across the wide river was just awesome. Once across the river I wished Brianne and the boys a great rest of their day. The tour guide rode off the route in search of his group to have some lunch and I pushed on in search of the welcome to Illinois sign. It did not disappoint.

I had missed a short cut though as I followed the route and all of the other cyclists went left along the river after their lunch. Brianne said they spilled out in Elizabethtown about 30 minutes before me, and that was with their break. I also had to stop and change my ninth spoke of the tour but hey I had ordered 50 more to pick up in Colorado and I had also finally rebuilt my other wheel, so I was covered. It had been fun trying to true a hand built wheel with my brake pads but it had worked after several hours of meticulously turning the spoke nipples.

I rode on after fixing the wheel and came across the town were Katie was spending the night. We had decided to do the same but it was not a great town to park an RV in. Brianne and I spent about 30 minutes in a gravel parking lot across from the gas station trying to decide where to go next. I told her I would ask the woman who ran the bed and breakfast where Katie was staying if she minded us parking outside of her place for the night. I rode out of the gravel and down the street to find her. She was kind enough to let me know the local sherif would not allow us to park off the street for the night but that there was an RV park along the river in the next town over. The town was off the route about three to four miles though, but that did not bother me so much as I was beginning to settle into the riding and cared less about what was on or off the route at that point.

The RV park along the river was quiet. It was small with full hookups. The view was extraordinary as each site was right against the river on a built up gravel pad. The camp host let Conor and Aaron ride around in his golf cart and promised s'mores by the camp fire at his spot later after it had gotten dark. It began to rain though as the sun went down and we had to take a rain check on the fire.

Illinois

The day started off grey with a light mist in Rosiclare, Illinois. The barges had crept by silently as we slept through the night and now I coasted off down the road silently while the town slept. I looked down at my cycle computer to see how many miles I had gone through town to get a good idea of when I would hit the T in the road which took me back onto the route. Unfortunately, my cycling computer had stopped registering miles and was sitting at zero. I had been removing it in the evening to keep it safe and dry in Isosceles with us but all the rain had corroded the contacts on the platform it clipped into. I played around with it and the bullet magnet which ticked of the wheel's rotations as it revolved past the sensor. It was a lost cause and so I embraced the fact that I might be shooting from the hip from then on when it came to knowing exactly where I was on the map in-between towns. The three to four miles back up to the route was a climb and the climbing continued on for another 17 miles after that. The rain kept up and I was wet and worn out by the time I reached the gas station in Eddyville, where I had planned on resting that morning.

Inside the young woman behind an old wooden counter asked me what I was looking for while I wandered around the store in search of a cheese Danish. I told her I was just browsing around and she replied, "We ain't got much." To this the gentleman at the table in front of the coffee pot laughed a bit and they went back to their morning ritual. I did find a cherry cheese bear claw and a cup of coffee. I paid the woman and stepped back outside to sit on the wet cement with my wet self to enjoy the little things in life. I sipped coffee and ate the pastry as Katie arrived. She pulled up along the building on the other side and leaned her bike against the wall before walking over and sitting down next to me. We sat outside the gas station for a bit to recover in semi-silence. I was not thinking too highly of the rest of the day, I told her, since my strength and or good attitude were sapped so early on. She went inside for some provisions and I followed adding a coke and some salt and vinegar chips to my meal. The vinegar chips really bite into the sides of my tongue and invigorate me, as long as I do not attempt to eat to many of them in one sitting. Katie went back to her bike after some more conversation and then I rested finishing my secondary snacks.

I finally set off again once I had the will to do so and Katie came around from the side of the building just as I was exiting the lot. The route changed up the hill and we both stopped there at the intersection to decipher which way we should go as there were no markings to explain which road was which. My Google Maps was of no help as my cell phone data was incognito at the moment. Katie had another carrier and was able to find the name of the road. We both took off down the hill and kept pace with each other for a while until another adventure cycling tour guide caught up with me. He and I slowed down to chat for about 20 minutes before he pedaled ahead to catch up with Katie. I caught up to them on some down hills as my weight gives me a great deal of advantage against lighter riders. We had a group ride for another 20 minutes before one of my rear spokes popped as we were whizzing around a turn leaving the main road for a smaller country one. I had learned at this point that large trucks passing by me or tight turns were some of the culprits for my spoke's early demise. I wished Katie and the guide safe travels as I coasted into the front end of someone's driveway for repairs.

I was now down to ten reserve spokes for that wheel until I reached Frisco, Colorado where 50 more awaited me at the post office by now. I was getting really quick at replacing them and truing the wheel. I really liked to find them broken on the hub side, as this saved me the time of deflating the tire, as I had mentioned before. This particular occasion did not disappoint. The owner of the home pulled up past me as I worked and gave me a glance, which I took as she was used to seeing random cyclists with their bikes flipped upside down in front of her home. I smiled at her and she went on inside as I finished my repair. I got back on the road and found many more hills were in my path. I was thoroughly burnt out and out of water by the time I reached the point where there was supposed to be a gas station, or so said my map. Well, I was running on the older version of the maps which were updated a month after I had ordered them, go figure. This was a correction I would have loved to have known about. I was still a few miles short of our lunch stop and very thirsty. I called Brianne when I finally got into town. She was fifteen minutes out and I rested on the curb of a Subway as I had marked it as where I would like to eat lunch that day. They have a wide selection of vegetables and sauces in which to make a tasty vegetarian sandwich with. The driveway into the restaurant was not so good for campers though and so I headed across the street to the discount store to buy soda and a snack. Katie ended up at the Family Dollar too just a bit after I had arrived. She told me that the guide was traveling on to meet his group at a Super Eight in the larger city further down the path. They were having a rest day tomorrow. He had invited her to join them for the evening but she had her eyes set on the lake area where we were to spend the night too. Our milage for the day would be about 10 to 20 miles shorter than the city and that was a good thing as far as my tired body was concerned. Brianne pulled in and we all headed over to

Subway. I got a huge veggie delight sub with every veggie they had! It was awesome and I was refreshed and renewed.

We headed back to the SUV just as it started to downpour. We sat in the dry comfort of the vehicle and rested for about an hour as the storm raged and then eventually passed. Katie waited inside the store were she reported it was a little too air conditioned for her liking. There were many puddles in the road as we wheeled out of town and the humidity picked up when the sun came back out. Katie and I rode past some farms and then the road quickly turned into rolling hills, which I had become really good at. I liked to really put an effort into the downhill pedal and then ride my momentum up the ascent coasting over the peak of the hill before repeating this lovely maneuver on the other side. I find the downhill exertion to be preferable to the long climb of the uphill. I left Katie behind here after the third such hill and soon found myself in Crabtree National Wildlife Refuge.

The ride through there was heavily shaded by trees and was mostly flat. It opened up to a large lake called Devil's Kitchen and that is where I went airborne over a huge bump in the road on a sharp downhill going over an old bridge. I enjoyed the thrill of leaving the ground but I imagine some of my spokes said a little prayer before I hit the pavement again, my tires bouncing hard. I stopped at the lake to rest and take in the surrounding beauty before heading on. I had hit rock bottom on my energy level for the day as I reached the dam road and realized Katie was right behind me again. I knew we were close to the campground that we had selected the night before but the last few miles of the day dragged on and on. I was ecstatic to see the turnoff when it finally appeared around a treed bend and coasted into the site that Brianne had picked out. I greeted my family and then sprawled out on top of the picnic table for a moment to rest.

Katie decided to stay next to the camper under some trees and gave Brianne some money to help with the cost of the site. We tried to give it back but she would not have it. She told us she was a C130 pilot in the Air Force and had been given the option to retire early. She had taken it and was now enjoying some epic adventures before settling into her new life out of military service. She was interested in flying commercial airliners and we hope to see her someday as we take a flight somewhere.

We all went down to the lake together and Katie swam out in her bicycle attire while Brianne and I splashed around with Aaron, Conor, and Gabriel. Katie told us this was one of the ways she had been doing laundry on the trip and I thought it was a great idea. Doug, a friend of ours back in Omaha, and I had washed up in a lake once while riding across Iowa and it had been one of those great experiences not everyone gets to have in life. The lake water is refreshing after a full day's ride and the sandy bottom feels so good as your toes sink into it. We would part ways with Katie in the morning as she had plans to head up the Lewis and Clark Trail through Omaha from there. Then she would travel over the Northern states to the same ending point in Astoria. I wondered if I would not have been tempted to linger too long in Omaha had I picked that route too. Brianne says she would never had let me but I can see how easy it would be to get into a routine once home again if we stayed more than a few days.

We rested out of the rain in the camper. The ground was muddy all around us but Katie had selected a good spot high enough with a pad of grass to keep it tolerable underneath her tent. Brianne made shepherd's pie for dinner with our veggie grounds, local produce, and instant mashed potatoes. My God it was good and just what my body had needed. Warm nourishment and rest were a great recipe for a good tomorrow. We would reach the border of Missouri in a town called Chester the next day.

I awoke around 6AM after sleeping in an hour later than normal. It felt good to just sleep in a little. Aaron was cuddled up to me and I snuggled him. The light began to slowly pour in through the skylight over the bed and I felt happy. Brianne began to stir and we all started to get out of bed. I went with Conor to the restrooms to brush our teeth and get ready for the day. Brianne scrambled farm fresh eggs, courtesy of Violet in Sebree, for us on tortillas with cheese and salsa. Katie had breakfast with us and after saying our goodbyes we wished each other well on our journeys. She was headed north through Saint Louis and we went west to the Ozark Mountain range.

The morning ride was dry, a first in a long while, and cool. I loved it for about two miles and then I was on the side of the road again replacing yet another spoke. I was getting low on spokes for this wheel now and still had a couple of states to cross before I was half way through the journey where I intended to replace the rear wheel with the one I had recently built. I took a wrong turn on my way into Carbondale. I guess I had missed the sign for the road I was supposed to be on but many roads were unmarked. A quick study of Google Maps set me down the right path again making use of another side road.

I Like to Ride

I eventually came to the outskirts of the city and turned right onto a feeder road for the main highway that went through this part of Carbondale. A young man crossed the street and walked towards me as I cycled into the city. "Do you have any cigarettes?" he asked. I informed him that I did not smoke. "Good for you!" he replied. I coasted on wondering if he was even old enough to smoke. I skipped the McDonalds up ahead as I was thinking their would be a Starbucks in Murphysboro but that was a mistake as there was nothing much on my route between there and the next city. The Starbucks had been in Carbondale, so Google Maps told me as I consulted it much too late. There was a decision to make in Murphysboro regarding the regular route versus the alternate route. The regular route had plenty of more hills whereas the alternate route went by the river and was flat for many miles. There was no way I was going to pass up some flat riding after all of the climbing I had been doing up until that day. So I turned left and went around the city on my way to the levee road. The route out to the flat part of the bypass was hilly but in a gradual up and down sort of way that does not bother one too much. There were a few turtles to save and then I was out in open farmland near the river where I came across the town of Gorham.

In Gorham I waited in the shade of the post office for Brianne and the boys to come and have lunch with me. I found the small town post offices to be a refuge from the sun as they almost all had an overhang of some sorts. There were no services in this town but a soda machine stood tall and proud near the post office. I sipped on a Mountain Dew as I sat on the cool pavement under the overhang. I had data coverage for my cell phone here in the middle of nowhere, which I found humorous as the coverage came and went with no regard to the size of the town I was in. There were no services for about 25 more miles and so I waited there to eat lunch. Brianne arrived and I noticed she had plussed up our supplies at Walmart in Carbondale. There were fresh chips! Salt and carbs, how they made the day so much better. After lunch I filled up three of my 32 ounce bottles and headed back out into the sun.

The wind had picked up then, much to my chagrin, and started to pound me in small but sapping gusts. I had a head wind to deal with and the flat open terrain made for very slow going. I came across a man from England who was eastbound having started in California making his way straight across the US. He was out on the flats too and having the time of his life with that great tailwind! He told me about the road ahead and what an adventure he had been having. I let him know about the road behind me, filled with great company like Sebree. The bad company too, like the dogs in the Appalachians. We parted ways with a wave. Further down the road I passed a pond with lily pads that looked vividly green and spectacular in the bright light of the partially cloudy day. It began to get a little warmer out then but not enough to bother me too much. The road passed fields of wheat ready for the harvest and I stopped to watch, no listen to them as they moved like a sea in the wind. They were beautiful golden rods of grain in the sun. The road turned from broken pavement into gravel as it passed an industrial looking operation where long conveyer belts high above the ground were taking something off to the river to be loaded onto barges. I turned down a one lane road and unintentionally played chicken with a truck as it flew through the area without a care. It took out a turtle, passing me up thank God. As I was climbing a sharp but short incline to another road there was that familiar twang as another spoke gave way. I could see all around as I was changing the spoke out, it was so flat out there. A man and a woman came up the road in their Jeep stopping next to me as I worked. "Do you want a ride?" the man asked. I told him I was about ready to put the repaired wheel back on and thanked him for the kindness he had offered. From there I stopped at a train crossing just as the arms came down to notify me of the train that was about to pass through. I took out my phone and took a video of it for our children who both love trains. After the train had passed I journeyed up the road to the main one that led to Chester, where we were to spend the night. The traffic picked up there and was mixed with cars, trucks, and motorcycles. I waved one handed to the latter as they passed me on the other side of the road and got mostly positive waves back. I did notice a change in the responses going from East to West. The further West I had gotten the less positive they were, if they responded at all.

Once on the main road there were a few mean hills left to conquer on my climb into Chester. I was thoroughly worn out by the time I topped the last of them and I rested in someone's front yard under a shade tree. I still had another mile and a half from there to the Benevolent Order of the Eagles lodge where Brianne and the boys were waiting in the cool air conditioning that Isosceles granted those blessed with hookups.

The Eagles lodge members had built a tiny bunk house, not unlike the ones in TroutDale. It was air conditioned too. Brianne had picked up the keys for it from the woman behind the bar at the lodge and she gave us the tour of the place to include the location of the showers. Noah and Brianna came into town about an hour behind me and stayed in the bunk house that night. I had a pitcher of Summer Shandy at the lodge and it really hit the spot. I ordered it thinking we would all share but found I was the only one in the mood for a drink that evening. I was parched and the beer was light, smooth, and refreshing. I did suffer from my lack of tolerance for such a large quantity of beer in such a short time though at this point in the trip. Brianna and Noah each had a pizza but there were no vegetarian options for us and so we unhooked our home from the SUV and drove to Dominoes for some cheese pizza. We took our pizza to the local laundry mat to get some much needed washing done. The laundry mat was extremely hot and humid. I felt like I was going to pass out chasing Aaron around as he got into all sorts of things. Aaron took me outside after a little while and across the street to the small memorial park in honor of Popeye the sailer. I did not know this until that day but Chester, Illinois was the birthplace of the creator of the popular television show.

Back at the camper I was beat from the long day. I was also not looking forward to the Ozark Mountain range that laid ahead of me in the morning. The Adventure Cycling guide had told me there were four days of epic hills. I would at least enjoy the scenery and try to remember that what goes up must come back down. Even if it was over and over again.

I Like to Ride

Missouri

The day started late as I slept in an extra hour. I heard Brianna and Noah leaving the bunk house just outside the camper and thought I should probably do the same as it was the first day of the Ozark Mountain Range and the slight reprieve I had from the hills on the levee was about to end in the foot hills of a mountain. I got everything packed up and headed outside to clean up in the outdoor restrooms that the Eagles had provided for us. After brushing my teeth and combing some beard oil through my mane I walked outside onto the sand volleyball court behind the lodge. There I consulted Google as to which path would be the best one out of town on my way back to the main route while ensuring I crossed paths with an egg biscuit and coffee establishment. I walked back across the parking lot which sloped down to where we were encamped, my sandal clips crunching and popping along the pavement as I strolled along. When I opened the door to Isosceles I found the boys sleeping next to each other on the left and Brianne cuddled up with Gabriel on the right. I wished them a great day and shut the door behind me. Google Maps was all programmed in now to take me where I wanted to go and I followed her voice, when I could hear it over the whirl of the wind my cycling was creating in the morning traffic. I zig zagged up side streets and into a back alleyway before reaching a main street with a Hardees on it. I knew this was just the breakfast stop I was in search of and parked my bike outside of the front door before entering. There were not too many people inside. Just two older gentleman to my right in the main dinning area. The woman running the counter smiled at me, "What can I get for you?" Her counterpart was filling the coffee thermos to my left and I ordered. I took a seat at the high top table and started sipping the hot coffee. This coffee was strong. I cut the bitterness with cream and sugar while I waited for my order to come up. The food ended up being much better than the coffee and it made for a good start to my day. I was really running behind by the time I leisurely strolled out of Hardees and brought Google Maps back up on my phone. Brianna and Noah were most likely way ahead of me by then and who knew if I would run into them again.

After leaving Hardees, Google was taking me downhill at a fast clip as I headed toward the river. I really should have thought that through as I soon found the error of my ways when I was routed to the base of the bridge that I needed to cross the river instead of the surface of it. I had to climb back up the same elevation to get to the main street in order to make my way to the entrance of the bridge. I cut through some roads that circled back and came upon a statue of Popeye who was waiting at the top to send me off across the Mississippi River. I just completed another state, albeit the small Southern tip of one, and now it was time for more adventure.

I was headed directly into the wind on a flat wide open road for a good hour after I passed the Missouri welcome sign. It was slow going and I could see the foothills of the Ozarks off into the distance. I knew there would be less wind under their cover but the climbing would begin and I really could not tell which of those would be harder. I was on a county road now and heading straight for the first hill. Large trucks were shaking the ground as they passed by me. I said a little prayer for my remaining original spokes and rode on. The first hill was steep and long as the foothill hills tend to be. I have come to believe that a cyclist has to pay their dues in the currency of elevation to get into a mountain range. The hills became more rolling after that and I was excited to find a gas station nestled near the crest of one, even though my map did not alert me to it.

I sat there for an hour on the pavement outside enjoying Gatorade, Mountain Dew, and the good company of the owner along with a clerk. The clerk gave me the cyclist journal they keep to read through and sign. Micheal had been there on the first of the month, five days before me, to rest as I now did. Steve and his group had been through too on their way east. Brianna and Noah were an hour ahead of me, the clerk reported. The clerk said Brianna came in, filled her water bottles, and departed. They must have been in a hurry. I met another couple heading eastbound while I rested there. Mark and Sue were on their way to Yorktown from California following route 66 for a good chunk of their journey. I warned them about the dogs in the Appalachians but they had a protective wrap around their tandem recumbent bicycle with a windshield in the front that looked dog proof to me. As long as they did not run into my little demon dog friend with the sharp teeth. I bid everyone a good day and headed back out and up the hill that led into the countryside.

The day got hot from there on out and I climbed steep grade after steep grade. The SPF50 sunblock stopped protecting me from the sun at some point and my arms burned. I caked it on until they were completely white but it was no use, the damage had been done. I kept on moving until I reached an empty church at a turnoff toward some town that was not on my route. I called Brianne and she told me to meet here at a distillery down the road a couple of miles where her and the boys were parked in the bus parking lot. I came across a stopped car in the middle of the road on my way there and the young occupants told me they were fine so I pedaled on. I was hot, sun burned, and tired when I came upon the Crown Valley Distillery. I wanted very badly for Brianne to spirit me away the last 13 miles into town but I rested there, eating salted chips and pickles, before I filled up my water bottles and headed back out into the sun. I really wanted to ride my bicycle across the country and not ride in the vehicle. I would use it though when we were done for the day to get back and forth to places with the family, when it was necessary for my health, and if I ever came across another person who wanted to assault me from their moving vehicle. I pedaled through the heat and ended up popping a spoke two miles before Farmington, where we were to spend the evening. I was too hot and burnt out to fix it there on the side of the road and so I spun on with a slightly wobbly rear wheel.

I finally came across Brianne and the boys at a park next to a church in the middle of the city. I pulled into the parking lot exhausted. There were several members of the church moving furniture and I watched them while I removed my helmet and sunglasses. Brianne and I talked over our overnight options and settled on the state park next to the city, as it was RV friendly and available. There was a highly recommended cyclist only home in town we could have stayed at called Al's place but it would have been difficult to park our trailer in the city. It felt great to pack up the bike and ride on to the St Joe State Park. That park ended up being one of the best RV sites we stayed at on the entire trip. We were thrilled with everything about the place from the personal greeting by the camp host as we were setting up to the low cost laundry facility and clean bathrooms. I wanted to stay there a couple of days and we could have since we really had no deadlines at that point but the road was a siren and she called to me. Later that evening we went into town for stuffed crust pizza but Conor got ill as we reached the restaurant and so we took it to go heading back to the camp site. We called it an early night and hoped Conor would feel better in the morning, as he usually did after such an illness.

It was a lazy morning the next day. We ended up giving Conor children's Tylenol after he got a light fever and cuddled him all night. The alarm I had set on my phone awoke me at 5AM and I let Gabriel use the great outdoors restroom before crawling back into bed. Brianne woke up about an hour later and wanted to know why I was not up and at em. I told her I had wanted to rest and so we looked at the maps and discussed what it would do to the schedule while the boys slept. We settled on a really late start and I went back to sleep.

It was great for a change to get up a little later around 7AM and be with my family most of the day. We went into Farmington for some spokes at the TransAm Cycle Shop and then stopped at Walmart to buy some athletic calf-high socks to cut into sun sleeves for my sunburnt arms. Brianne had suggested that I use the socks as an additional protection and they worked great. Conor was feeling much better at this point and we headed back to the camp site to pack up. At 3PM Brianne kicked me out onto the route and I began to pedal my way to Centerville.

The ride started at a slight uphill and into the wind. I was sad to have to go 46 miles so near the end of the day but after about an hour I was in my groove. I found Brianne and the boys playing in a park by an old battlefield at Pilot Knob. I stopped in to say hi, playing with the kids for a while. I hit the rode again passing a cafe that I would have stopped in for breakfast had it been earlier in the day. I turned down another road and into a good headwind, the pedaling became slow. There was a McDonalds up in the distance and I promised myself an egg and cheese biscuit upon reaching its golden arches. Well, apparently they do not serve said biscuits so late in the day. I passed on dinner and made my way back out into the wind. About a mile down the road the route turned left crossing the busy evening traffic. I am not a big fan of left turns on busy roads, when I must make my way from the far right and cross paths with hurried motorists. The oncoming traffic did not slow down for me and so I had to pedal quickly to make it through them.

The road began to go up and down from there and I got back into mountain climbing mode. There were some great downhill runs and even a self propelled roller coaster for a decent stretch where I was able to again pedal hard down the hill and coast up the next. Some bad grades started to appear that felt like enormous waves as I leaned back riding up to their crest. I could see the tops of these unlike the Appalachian Mountain switchbacks giving me hope that I could make it. The day ended well as I pulled into Centerville faster than I had expected at sometime around 7PM. We were boondocked again, this time in front of the courthouse on a side street. Brianne had cooked up a large pot of pasta. I helped her drain the water on the lawn as the town held a meeting outside of the courthouse doors. We had cleared our stay with the local sheriff who was in an office on the right of the courthouse. There was another gentleman who rode in as the sun set and he parked his bicycle along the shops that lined the street across from our camper. He sat on a wooden bench removing his socks to rub his sore feet before retreating into his apartment. Tomorrow was to be the worst of the Ozarks according to the Adventure Cyclist guide I had met while waiting to cross the ferry into Illinois. From there it was just the upper gaps left in the range and then the sweet descent into Kansas where the eyes could look deep off into forever.

The next day I started off early to conquer the worst ascents the mountains had to offer before it got too crazy hot outside. I quickly ate the cold oats and powdered milk that Brianne had put together for me the night before and hit the open road. There was little traffic in these parts of the Ozarks and I spent most of the morning climbing and then going back down as I had been doing the days leading up until then. One hill was particularly long that morning but there was a gas station at the top where I stopped for a sticky bun and some heavily creamed coffee. I doctored all of my coffee at this point for the benefits of making it heavy on the caloric intake and to cut the bitterness or strengthen the weakness. At one point during the climb a bee circled my head for over a mile, threatening me repeatedly. I thought my beard oil had attracted it until I became agitated enough to stop and see if I could persuade it to knock it off without getting stung. I was surprised to discover it was a horse fly and then I realized it had been after a quick meal. Good thing I was not on the menu that day.

Later, around Eminence, I came across Brianna and Noah. They were at the ATM sitting along the side of the road. It was at the top of the hill and I swung in to say hello. They had spent the evening around there having passed through Centerville the day before. It felt good to have caught back up with them and I rode behind on the way to Alley Spring. The ride from there took us up a major hill and the heat of the day really set into my back as the sun made my skin crawl. We went up and then we went down in a roaring blur reaching speeds of around 42 miles per hour. Brianna would later tell us that this was the fastest she had ever gotten up to on her bicycle. I think it was about the same for me at the time although I had never kept track before I installed a cycling computer. There had been one really long drop of a hill on the last day during my ride across Iowa two years before this and it had felt similar. I like to lean in really low into the handle bars raising my back and rear end into a flat line. I can feel the vibration and micro wind generated from the front wheel as it spins faster and faster. The wind zips into my eyes tearing them up as I go. The threat of pain and death are always at the back of the mind as I glide to the sunken bottom of the descent.

We were in Alley Spring now and I broke off from the small pack we made to meet up with Brianne and the boys at the mill. The parking lot was full of cars, vans, and a bus. There was a rapid stream rushing behind some picnic areas and off into the distance I saw children playing around a pavilion. I parked the bike next to Isosceles and walked down the lot towards the pathway that led to the mill. Conor came running up to me and I caught him in my arms. He gave me a kiss and then Aaron and Brianne followed with Gabriel. We all had lunch in the parking lot as they told me about their adventures at the mill. After lunch I bid them farewell for the afternoon and walked over to a shade tree to nap for a spell. It was still repressively hot out and the stream sounded peaceful. Brianna and Noah arrived and rested there too with me but soon left as they were motivated to end their day. A group of kids and some parents arrived where I rested and wanted to use the picnic area next to the tree I was under. I gladly gave it up and started to pack up for the final stretch of the day when one of the parents asked, "Would you like some oranges and summer sausage?" I jumped at the chance to pack up two fresh oranges but politely turned down the meat. I wished them a great day and then coasted out of the parking lot and directly into the toughest ascent of the route through those mountains.

The climb out of Alley Spring was evil at this time of the day. It was really hot and the sun was very harsh on the road well outside of the shade. I could feel my heart racing to keep up with what I was demanding of my body and it felt like it was in the red by the time I reached the top. I stopped for a moment to rest while the pounding of my heart rang throughout my ears. I did not stay long though as there was rest to be had on the descent as well.

I caught back up with Brianna and Noah in the last five miles before Summerville where we had all planned to spend the night. Brianne found a youth center with some cabins that we could park alongside to run water and power out to Isosceles. The place was inexpensive and had a small playground for the boys to play on. Brianna and Noah camped out at the city park about a quarter mile from our location. The sun set as Brianne cooked dinner and the boys played.

I skipped breakfast the next day to get on the move. The forecast called for heat, open sky, and wind in the afternoon. I was really beginning to understand the drill now with the wind. It was light in the morning and picked up by early afternoon when the real heat was on. Brianne called out to me for the car keys as I started to ride off. I was glad she caught me because it would have been a long day riding back and forth to deliver the keys. The morning was cool and the hills were mere shadows of the mountains I had climbed through the day before. I put 26 miles behind me by 9AM and the only downer was a motorist yelling at me to get out of the road as they zoomed by me at 60 miles per hour. I found it amusing that my presence bothered them so much as it did not impede their driving. I popped yet another spoke as a heavy gravel truck passed me. Poor road surfaces and heavy trucks were the bane of my rear wheel's existence. I completed the last six miles of the ride into Houston before I fixed it as I had started to become less worried about them at this point. I changed them when a more advantageous time presented itself.

There was a McDonalds a little off the route in the larger town of Houston and it was most assuredly egg and cheese biscuit time. I enjoyed the hot coffee and the wifi before I sat outside and fixed the spoke. I was able to fill my water bottles with ice and cold water which really made for a better riding experience. I trued the wheel and headed out down the road. I saw a sign that read 32 miles to Fort Leonard Wood. This is were I was sent for basic training in 1999 when I had enlisted into the Army as an 88M, heavy wheel operator.

I passed just underneath the base on the path that day and might have stopped in had it not been a days ride off the route. The afternoon was hotter but I was riding fast as the wind was mostly blocked by the shade trees along the road. I pulled into the cross roads of a town called BenDavis and stopped at the store on the side of the road. A young boy opened the door for me and handed me a cyclist journal. I leafed through it looking for familiar names but found none. I signed my name after a few remarks and went to the restroom to wash my hands and face. There was a woman in the back making pizza as I passed to enter the restroom. "Don't drink the tap water. It's full of heavy metals," she warned as I entered. I thanked her for the warning and saw what she was talking about in the stains the water had left on the surfaces it touched. I cleaned up and walked out to find some food. There were all sorts of sodas, teas, and good things to pick for lunch. The woman from the back came out and filled my water bottles from a gallon jug of distilled water. I thanked her and sat down at the table near the window. People started to come in filling the store to capacity. I picked a great time to stop in as a group of neighbors from around the area were gathering to have lunch and talk. They told me that they normally came on a different day of the week but had changed their meeting to that day. I really enjoyed the conversation and was offered hot homemade scones and stories about the area. I told them of my experiences with the military and about the journey so far. Brianna and Noah stopped in and Noah took my picture with everyone. I thanked them for their kindness and then picked up my things.

I rode out with a full tummy and high spirits. Brianne and the boys were waiting for me a mile down the rode at a church and I stopped in for hugs and kisses. Brianna and Noah rode past us waving as they went by and I smiled back with a mouth full of fresh strawberries. I soon followed taking off for the last 26 miles into Hartville. There were more aggressive hills but not too bad. I caught back up with Brianna and Noah and we formed a pack again for the last part of the day.

Hartville had a beautiful city park on a lake with RV hookups for $10 per night. We payed the county clerk across from the courthouse and went back to settle in. Air conditioning and a beautiful view goes a long way towards making a comfortable campsite. I washed my cycling jersey and pants under the outdoor shower on the camper and then took Brianne to the library so she could update the website in peace. The boys and I had ice cream from a gas station and talked with Grandma and Grandpa on the phone before we picked up Brianne a couple of hours later. We then dropped our camper and headed to the next town over to have dinner with friends we had spoken to through our work with Ohtahara Syndrome. They were very kind and bought us dinner at a Mexican restaurant. We love Mexican food and the night was very fun and relaxing. I also scoped out where my breakfast was going to come from in the morning. We were headed to the last overnight town in Missouri the next day, AshGrove. There was a kind woman at the city hall there who had promised a place to stay and a pool.

Their was a fog in the Ozarks as I departed the city park by the lake. It was truly a beautiful morning. There was a climb out of Hartville and near the top there was a dead fox in the road. It was both sad and beautiful to me curled up where it had been hit by a car. It must have rested there from its mortal wounds before passing on. There were many fast moving cars on the way to Marshfield. We had seen the aftermath of a roll over accident on that route the evening before on the way to dinner and I could see that this was most likely a regular occurrence around there with the way people were driving. I ended up in the morning rush but made it through safe and in good time.

I had breakfast and topped my water bottles off with ice before hitting the road to Fair Grove. The day started to get hot fast and I cooled off with an icee from a busy gas station. A retired sheriff whose son had also made the same journey across the US told me that he was working for a program in Philadelphia that puts together tours which work on Habitat For Humanity builds along the route. It made my heart glad to hear of such a cool project for young men and woman to embark on before settling into careers. Brianne and the boys met me for lunch and we enjoyed egg salad sandwiches made fresh that morning by Brianne. I was getting a large amount of protein for the day and loved it.

After lunch I was off to conquer the remaining hills and heat of the day. The hills proved to be formidable and they kept coming the rest of the afternoon. None of them rivaled the hills of Eminence and Alley Spring though. I was very happy to pull into Ash Grove where there was a pool and a house waiting for us as promised. Ash Grove was on a mission to support Trans-American cyclists. There was a large park, basketball court, parking lot with hookups for Isosceles, and a large home which Brianne had picked up the keys for earlier. I walked over to the home to see what was inside when a man approached us wondering, "Are those my keys? Let me take a look at them." Apparently he had lost the keys to his shed and thought we had made off with them. He was the city grounds keeper and you could tell he was not as receptive to cyclists as the rest of the population there. "Can you move your friends tent over there too? It's in the grass and I need to mow." We assured him that we had no idea who the tent belonged to and were just going to get settled in. I drove the camper around to a good spot out of the way in the parking lot and hooked up to the 20 amp circuit at the light post. I went into the home and showered. The cold water felt so awesome on my warm dusty skin. Once I was clean I started cooking dinner in the kitchen. There was a lived in feel to the home as cots and personal belongings filled the main room. The room off to the side was open and I made a mental note to let Brianna and Noah know should they stop in for the night.

A young woman from Israel showed up as I was cooking dinner and told me that she had just finished serving in the Israeli Army. She had read about the TransAmerican Trail and thought it sounded like an epic challenge for her to embark on. Her group had been hold up there in that house for four days as one of their party rested an injured knee. I told her of my overuse injury in the Appalachians and she warned me not to press my luck with such injuries in the future. I imagined she was right to stop and rest until it had healed because mine did not do so until I also had rested it. She started out on May 9 and was also westbound. I finished cooking our dinner of pasta and vegetables and wished her safe travels. We offered dinner to Brianna and Noah as they arrived while we were dishing up under a pavilion but she was a cook and had plans to go shopping in town making full use of the kitchen. The home was a kind of hub for cyclists as it and the lawn outside filled up during the evening. We slept well that night knowing that the next day we would be on our way to Pittsburg, Kansas. We would meet up with some old friends and go to Napoli's for dinner.

I Like to Ride

The restaurant where my dream of this journey was truly sparked into being. I was stoked!

Kansas

I kicked off the day right as the sun was coming up and I am glad I did as it had been getting warmer out earlier in the day. The morning provided me with the last dying gasps of the Ozark Mountain Range. Their great hills faded into the dust behind my tires as I spilled out into the plains. Flat open roads gave me a cruising speed of around 20 miles per hour, aided by a slight breeze at my back. I zoomed into a golden city lit by the ever rising sun. I was on empty water bottles and searched out a place to refill them. To my surprise there was a cafe with an awesome breakfast right there smack dab in the middle of no where! I parked my bike along the brick wall in front of the place and entered. There was a man behind the long old cafe style counter cooking short order with his back to me. A waitress was filling coffee at a nearby table and I could see the place was popular. The tables were all full save the darker back end. I walked to the counter and waited for the man to finish what he was doing before speaking, asking him if I could order and eat outside. I had been hard at work out there in the growing heat of the intense sun and was more than dripping with perspiration. The man laughed, "You are more than welcome to eat in here if you like!" I did like and so I walked back to the table just on the edge of the darker part of the restaurant taking my seat and waiting to order. The waitress came bearing gifts of water and coffee. I took greedily of both as I ladled on the cream and sugar making the black coffee a light sweet brown. She also brought me the cyclist journal and a menu to look over. I was very hungry and the smell of short order breakfast filled the air. I ordered biscuits, jam, pancakes, eggs, hash browns, and a side of toast. Did I go over board? Yes, yes I did. The journal had unfamiliar names in it but there was a common thread to it. "Make sure you eat the pie." Once the food came, I ate my large order until I was satiated. My only regret is that I did not save room for pie which Cooky's Cafe was most famous for on the route. I am happy to report the rest of the food was top notch even without the pie. I had to drag myself out of there as I was filled to the gills. The waitress had packed me two full water bottles along with ice for the hard day ahead of me. These kind gestures by complete strangers touched my heart.

The next 33 miles were tough ones. The ice cold water quickly became warm in the harsh heat of the day. I had just enough water to make it to Pittsburg, Kansas but the cross and head winds slowed me down considerably along with sapping my internal water supply. I still averaged 14 miles per hour but it took its toll on my body and I ended up falling asleep behind a farmer's shed. It had been the only shade I could find and I was not going to make it much further without a rest. A few trucks past by me as I sunk in and out of sleep in that blissful shade. I lingered in that place where you are not awake but easily stirred. After 40 minutes I awoke and willed myself back out into the sun to finish the last 14 miles.

I caught my second wind as I came across the Kansas border, which was good because I had several more miles to bike once inside of the city as it was a larger one than usual. I entered through the side of the city where there was an office I had once worked at installing a network in the middle of the night. It had been sold since and there was not much out around this part of the city other than a gas station. I girded myself against stopping just yet and kept moving towards main street and the downtown area were I knew there would be a coffee shop. I came across an awesome coffee shop with milkshakes, espresso, and wifi. The good kind of wifi too, not that token wifi that does not carry enough bandwidth for more than one or two people to share. I sat outside in the shade at one of their small tiled and rounded tables. My back was to the store and I looked out across the main street as people bustled around enjoying their late afternoon. I also uploaded some pictures to the our website and rested there for an hour. Brianna and Noah arrived after a while and told me Noah had broken a spoke. I certainly could relate. They headed off to the bike shop and I went to Walmart to meet up with our friends Vanessa and Isaac.

Once we found each other we talked in the shade at the back of the Walmart while we waited for Brianne and the boys to arrive from seeing her relatives nearby in Joplin, Missouri. While we talked a gentleman by the name of Ernest walked over and we found out he had a passion for cycling. He liked hybrid bikes just like mine for their comfort and I have to agree that they do have that advantage. He had been on many long rides and we spoke of the dangers of the heat and dehydration. I really enjoyed meeting him and was very thankful for the money he gave us to stay at an RV park in town. Isaac bought us all ice cream, to include Ernest. Another gentleman approached and wanted to talk. He was homeless and had been wandering America for some time now. He used to serve in the Marines and had also biked across most of America making his way from town to town in search of a life free from societal burdens. We wished each other well on our journeys and he walked back over to the intersection to resume panhandling.

Brianne called and we all agreed to meet her at an office parking lot made available to us. They had run an electric cord outside of the building so we would have power but we feared using it since it was so hot out and running the air conditioner on a light duty cord was a risk that we did not want to take.

Daniel McDonald

The sun was really beating down on the parking lot and when Brianne arrived we moved on to the RV park. There were other cyclists staying in tents at the small park. One couple from Germany was sunburnt from the ride I had just been through. They had taken several days there to recover and would most likely not be leaving in the morning as I was going to. The park was just what we needed as it had showers, water, electricity, and was on the route, which added to my happiness level. After setting up camp we all set out to have dinner at Napoli's. We had an Italian feast leaving us leftovers if you can believe it. I drank four pitchers of ice water, ate three pieces of pizza, and an order of cheese ravioli. It was everything I had dreamt it would be.

Once back at camp we filled Isosceles' fresh water tank while Vanessa and Isaac's children played with Aaron and Conor around the parking lot. Thanks to Ernest my family was sleeping in comfort that night.

Left over pizza was on the menu for breakfast the next morning. I spun down the road leaving the city behind me as the sun cast a hazy pink light in the sky. It was Sunday and there was little to no traffic. I crossed a strange site along one set of fence posts where there were countless mummified catfish heads, jaws gaping wide as they swallowed the posts. That was a first. Later down the road I came across the small town of Girard and turned into a gas station for a Mountain Dew slurpy along with some snack cakes. I ate outside at a small table and watched the traffic go by until I was ready to leave. The road was closed heading in the direction of my travel from there and so I turned out into oncoming traffic and then into the closed portion of the road. I was not worried about the torn up road but should have at least looked around before making such a move as I did so right in front of the town sheriff! There was nothing left to do but smile and wave and so I did. Thankfully it was reciprocated.

The morning turned out to be hot, humid, and I was coated in sweat. I had started before 6AM though and was making good time in the least hot part of the day. I met back up with Brianna and Noah a few miles after Girard and rode with them most of that day. We separated in Chanute as I met up with Brianne and the boys at Walmart. Lunch was awesome. Egg salad on tortillas with fresh tomatoes. The sun really started to beat down on me after lunch though and I came across a dust devil on a lonesome gravel rode. I stopped to watched it for a few minutes as it swirled and danced across the dirt. It passed through me whipping up dust everywhere around me. I then pressed on into the endless and shadeless void keeping my arms tucked in close to my body to keep them out of the sun as much as possible. Then I heard a twang and felt the wobble of a tired spoke releasing itself from the stress of our journey together. It took me about 15 to 20 minutes to replace it with the relentless sun baking me as I worked. I was careful not to make any mistakes in my movements as I wanted to be back in my own self propelled breeze as soon as humanly possible. I flipped the bike back over and loaded it once the job was finished. I raised my warm water bottle into the air to drench my face and mouth. Then I hit the road again pedaling onward into the dusty hot afternoon.

I finally came across the turnoff to the town of Benidect. It was the place where we were to meet up with my parents that evening. We had finally come to the point in our journey where my mother had said she would join in on the fun. She had purchased a camper van for the trip and my father had decided to accompany her at the spur of the moment just before she left Omaha. I found Benidect to be a sleepy town removed from the main road. I stopped in at the general store but it was closed. There was a soda machine out front and I bought a cold drink to sip on while I waited for Brianne and the boys. As I sat there I noticed the spinal column of some long deceased animal laid out on a wooden picnic table. Sometimes I just get weirded out by seeing something like that. Once it happens I just need to move on and so when Brianne pulled in I let her know I was ready to push on further down the road before we finished out the day. We filled my water bottles and I pulled on my sun guards to prepare myself. There was no cell phone coverage in the town so Brianne would have to find some in order to let my parents know where the new rendezvous point would be.

Google Maps had just enough information to show me that I could pedal through town and back onto my route instead of backtracking a couple of miles and so I moved forward. Once back out on the main road the temperature suddenly dropped around 15 degrees. It felt so wonderful to catch a short break from the super heated air. There were farmers off in the distance harvesting wheat and the debris floated in the wind up and around me on its flight away from the coming storm. Suddenly strong winds flanked me from the left. I had to lean into them to stay upright on the bicycle. Large bolts of lighting started to strike off into the distance sending loud claps of thunder that began to come sooner and sooner after each flash. I pedaled on as the farmers rushed now to harvest their wheat before it became drenched by the storm. The air was full of dust now and the wind kept coming on harsher than before. Brianne had posted up the road at my next turn to make sure I would not miss it. I had a quick decision to make once there whether I should catch the tailwind of this beast and ride it out or hitch a ride taking me further down the road and hopefully out of the storms path. I jumped in the vehicle with her after tossing the bike into Isosceles. We zoomed down the small back road a few miles and then turned off into another small town where I jumped out and got back on the bike with haste. I was on the edge of the storm now and looked to have bought some time to complete the day at the state park further down the way. We spent the next hour with Brianne driving up ahead and me pedaling to meet her as we tried to find the correct route to the camp ground. The rain began to fall on me and Brianne called me to say that the sheriff had stopped her to let her know a powerful storm was heading in her direction. I was soaked and completely frustrated at this point. We grouped back up and then drove through a cemetery where either the road had run through it or the dead had surrounded the road.

The woman at the entrance to Cross Timbers State Park showed us where to go for RV camping and we moved to our final destination for the evening just as the sun began to set and the storm finished blowing through. There was electric and water hookups and two spots available next to each other, which was handy since my parents were meeting us there in about an hour. We set up camp and worked on drying my clothes out. Brianne put dinner on since my parents had already stopped to eat theirs and we settled in.

It was a wonderful place to meet up. The trees surrounded the camp sites and the lake was a nice touch off in the distance.

We all hugged each other when my parents arrived. I helped them park and hook up for the night. They had also brought our resupply and we got busy transferring it from their camper van into our storage. Orion, their dog, and Gabriel started the process of getting acquainted with each other and we watched them, a little nervous about what displays of dominance might occur. My parents did not sleep well that night as they were just beginning to adjust to nights on the road. We slept well though and woke up late the next day. I dreamt of the Rocky Mountains that lay a state ahead waiting for me.

In the morning I passed through the Flint Hills. The gradual grades went on and on into the distance for as far as my eyes could see and there was a haze on the horizon all morning. The plains in the Flint hills were like a vast sea of cattle, wheat, and corn. You could pedal on for hours upon hours without end. I did eventually end up at a Sonic in Eureka. I just had to stop for a crushed ice lime aid. There is something very satisfying about a sweet tart drink when you are flush from working long hours in the heat. It cuts right through your thirst. I put down a very large one, biggest one they had in fact. It hit the spot. From there the day went on into the sun and then the bright rays softened a little under some fresh cloud cover. I pedaled on and on through those hills.

At some point later in the day I came to where the route split from the hills and headed into the less traveled places. A short distance down the road from the turn was a very small town. I rested at their post office which lay 19 miles from Cassoday where we were all going to meet up for the evening. The woman who operated it let me use the faucet out back to fill my empty water bottles. She had wanted to let me behind the counter to use the sink but was afraid she might be caught and lose her job. It was understandably, of course, against their regulations to allow a complete stranger next to everyone's mail. I let her know I fully understood and was content with hose water.

The water was cool and felt good as I drank deeply with abandon. I walked around the wood sided building to the front where there was more shade to be had and plopped down cross legged under the large awning. I almost fell asleep there as my mind drifted in the silence of their empty main street. I dug through my panniers a little and produced a bag of pickle flavored potato chips. The salty chips gave me a little boost as I munched and starred out across the street taking in the small buildings around me. I noticed the American flag on one of them was blowing briskly in the direction of my travels. I smiled as I picked myself up not wanting to miss such an opportunity. A woman pulled up to the post office then and asked me if I needed anything. Such kindness from a stranger. I almost felt bad that I did not need anything at that moment. She let me know that the church down one block from where I had come was open and I could use it to rest if I liked. I have found the churches along the route to be filled with compassion. I thanked her for her kindness and hopped back on the saddle to finish out the day. From the shade of the post office awning I shot out onto the plains under the hot sun carried by a very energizing tailwind.

I was now doing a good 19 to 22 miles per hour with little effort and it was an amazing change of pace from the slower speeds I had become accustomed to. The road went on forever into rural fields. I cruised along until it curved to the left and then went on again for a long time. The road curved right once more and I could make out the outline of some buildings far off into the distance. The wind carried me and I flew into Cassoday in just under an hour from the moment I left the post office. I rested there on an old wooden bench in front of a closed up shop in the shuttered downtown main street. Cassoday had seen busier days in the past I was sure but I am unhappy to report it lays dormant as of 2016. We all met up around an hour later and made camp in the old city park. It was tucked away in a small wooded area near a creek on the other side of town. My parents pulled in between some trees and started up their generator to get some air conditioning going. We set up Isosceles in the circle at the end of the dirt road near the picnic tables and outhouse. The outhouse was not very friendly looking and we were thankful for our cassette toilet in the camper. There was a hidden hydrant in the woods that we used to fill our water and a gazebo with power for our phones. There were also legions of nymphs, baby ticks, which made for an evening of pulling them out of everyone and from everywhere. Brianna and Noah stopped in for the night as well. A local teen came racing into camp on his mountain bike and stopped abruptly by turning it sideways and then sliding out. He walked up to the outhouse and disappeared inside for a minute. He then exited and proceeded to sit down at the picnic table next to Brianna where he started up a conversation with her about anything and everything. You could tell he liked her and liked the company of the rest of us outsiders. He asked me to check out his bike and I noticed that he had no brakes. This accounted for the irregular way in which he had stopped it earlier. He said he wished he could leave Cassoday but that his grandparents would not allow him to. I told him that he should fix his brakes and ride out of town on the TransAmerican Trail as soon as he graduated high school. That the world was out there just waiting for him to explore. I truly hope he did. That night I slept like the dead and the ticks feasted.

The morning started off early as I had large amount of territory to cover in-between services. I did end up taking a wrong turn out of the park as I thought I knew which direction the route was but apparently was wrong on that account. I had learned to be leery of which way I was headed by then in the journey though and stopped to consult the map and Google just to be sure. I corrected my course a block down the road. After that it was nothing but cross wind and slow pedaling as I fully woke up over the next 40 miles. The road was lined with tall brown grass that had gone to seed and I rode the bicycle next to it allowing the small stocks to brush against my right leg every now and again. I imagine I was inviting another tick feast in doing so but it was too good of an experience to pass up. It was therapeutic to be out there alone with the wind and the grass. The sun was a huge red ball slowly rising, painting the sky as it went, and turning the grass into gold. The air was much cooler than it would be in several hours allowing me to work the pedals hard. I drank in my vast surroundings and was at peace.

After an endless stretch I came across a town with a Braum's ice cream parlor on its outskirts. I soon realized with delight that I had been there once before on business. I got a kick out of that as I pulled in to enjoy some hot breakfast. The girls behind the counter were preparing for the day as I starred at the menu board looking for my biscuits and eggs. I found them and some vegetarian bagel combination too. I added coffee and hash browns along with a double dipped mint chocolate chip sugar cone. Then I walked over to the cream and sugar station by the soda machines to doctor up my coffee before sitting down to wait for my food to come up. There was a group of children eating breakfast at the table in front of me, no doubt before heading off to some fun summer activity. There was also a gentleman and his son enjoying lite conversation as they filled up for the morning as well. I walked back over to the counter to see if my food was ready and found it was not. I waited there for a moment. The manager asked if she could help me, thinking that I was not being helped out quickly enough, but I assured her that I was well taken care of. A moment later my food was up and I rushed it back over to the table where I had left my coffee at. I put a fair amount of salt on things and began to enjoy my breakfast. The weather forecast was on the television above the soda machines letting me know just how hot things were going to get over the next few days. I was super excited to ride all day long in 100 plus degree weather. No, I was not. I knew I would need to keep waking up very early to accomplish my daily goal of pushing at least 80 or more miles. I polished off my breakfast and drank more coffee than I should have. I cleaned up the table sweeping the grains of salt into my hand and took the trash over to the receptacle. Then I was off to Heston with a huge dose of caffeine coursing through my veins!

I rode through the rest of town heading down their busy main street and finally spilling back out into the rural fields on the other side. I had crossed paths with a few other cyclists who were out running errands and was happy to see such a great use of an economical form of transportation. I had not seen much of this back in Omaha. I passed a woman transporting her child by bicycle and trailer from one town to the next. They were both out enjoying the sun and smiled at me as I announced my presence before riding by on their left. The route turned right from there and then after another stretch I made it into Heston. From there I rode through town, stopping to rest by a row of industrial looking businesses on its edge before heading on to Buhler. Once there I rested under a tree just outside of an empty school waiting for Brianne, the boys, and my parents. The day had grown very hot and the sun was about at full strength. A squirrel played off to my left and I talked with him for a spell. He did not seem to mind the company and continued to run around the trees next to me.

When my family arrived it was lunch time in the air conditioning of the camper van. I decided I was going to go another 19 miles to Nickerson mostly because the cool air and full belly gave me a false sense of strength. As we ate our meal the lead rider, Steffen Streich, in the TransAmerica Race rode past at an easy stroll of a pace. He looked lean and light as he just coasted by in the shimmering heat. I imagined he was just keeping the bike moving in order to generate a breeze while not overexerting himself. Brianna and Noah later told tell me that he had stopped to speak with them on the side of the road as they crossed paths. They learned about the website that tracked the riders' positions in the race and followed the action from there on out.

The last stretch of the day was not so much fun. It was super hot and a nasty head wind caught me right after leaving the parking lot. I toiled hard under the hot sun to reach Nickerson. The road passed by a farm with zebras and I stopped to watch them as I rested. I also popped a spoke a mile out from town and chose not to fix it until after I met back up with everyone for the evening. I took a few wrong turns after that trying to find the route through town and came across a gas station. I went inside and filled up on salty nachos drenched in orange cheese then topped it all off with a 44 ounce Mountain Dew. I called Brianne and she headed over to pick me up to take me to the RV park in Sterling. The evening was fun filled as Sterling turned out to be a really great town with an awesome pool right next to the RV park. The town was a ways off the route and I would be pedaling those extra miles the next day to get back but it was so worth it. We swam in the pool and had dinner outside on the picnic bench in between our campers. My mother had cut up fresh fruit and made a salad while Brianne cooked pasta in tomato sauce. Full hookups gave us cool air and a lower humidity had moved in which made for a very comfortable evening.

I started off the next morning super early. It was dark and the RV park was dead quiet as I rode down the gravel to the restrooms. The sound of the rocks crunching under my tires echoed off the RV's. I pulled up to the men's side of the restrooms and opened the door to find a gentleman heeding nature's call. I apologized for the intrusion and waited outside for him to finish up. The lock on the door had broken and I imagine made for many awkward moments over the days since it had stopped working. Once my teeth were clean and my face was fresh I switched on the rear blinker and front headlight on my bicycle before I rode off down the road back through the empty downtown. It was a bit of a ride to get back to the route but it was straight from there and had only one turn that I needed to ensure I did not miss. I kept my eyes peeled for it as I had no intention of adding anymore miles to the day than necessary. Once I found it I turned right heading down the smaller country side road. I passed by a massive flock of birds circling in the now hazy morning light. There was then a large stretch of miles to traverse without services for water or food. I did come across a yard with a hose sticking outside of the fence with as sign that read "Water for cyclists." I really thought that was kind but could not make use of it since I was on the beginning of the long haul and my bottles were still full. The morning ride was endless from there on. It was only broken up by a popped spoke, which I stopped to repair outside of a lone farmhouse. The mosquitos quickly swarmed me as I worked forcing me to quicken the pace of my repairs. It was the fastest spoke switch out so far for me on the journey and I was really glad to be back in a self made breeze that kept the vampires at bay. I soon rode into Quivira National Wildlife Refuge and it was beautiful in the morning light. I came across another cyclist heading eastbound towards the middle of the preserve and we stopped to chat for a while. Joe was heading from San Francisco to Yorktown. He thought it was very strange that there were oil wells in the wildlife refuge, we both had seen them in passing, and I joked with him that they needed to get it from everywhere to include protected places. It is kinda strange to pump oil out of the ground in a refuge though and I hope there is never a spill as it was so beautiful.

I went through several sore joints and muscles over that long 52 mile stretch and ran out of my 128 ounces of water just as I was a mile out from Larned. I found a cafe on main street and stopped in for coffee and some breakfast. The walls of the cafe were covered in a local woman's art and the pictures told a story of solitude on the prairie. I wondered if they portrayed the feelings she had as a young woman growing up in rural America. Breakfast was good, I had blueberry pancakes, and the map told me there were about 32 miles left to Rush Center were we had planned to finish the day. The sun was up high in the sky now though and it was hot as an oven. The waitress helped me fill my water bottles with ice and cold water before I left for the pain and suffering ahead of me.

The next 32 miles did end up being very difficult as the temperatures soared into the 100s. I stopped in at the Fort Larned museum to fill my water bottles again as I was draining them very quickly. I spent an hour there cooling off in the air conditioning, which the curator told me was broken and blowing nonstop. What a God send to have it malfunctioning in such a positive way for a roasted traveler such as myself. I bought two bottles of orange cream soda and we chatted about the history of the fort and all the other cyclists who had stopped in over the years. She had me put a pin in the map for Omaha. I thanked her for her hospitality and went back out into the nightmare of a hot day. I rode down the road for some time before turning off onto another road catching a tailwind. The wind took me the last 20 miles but it felt like being inside of an oven.Tailwinds are great for achieving maximum speed but they create a bubble of dead air around you and when the air stops moving you really feel the full effect of the temperature. I was zooming at 22 miles per hour but was cooking too. I felt sick from the heat and began to pour water over my head to keep it cool. It was a massive waste but felt necessary at the time. I pushed through as there was no shade out there to rest in and no traffic to flag down should my body fail in the heat. I made it out the other side just as my water ran out. I sought refuge in the small park where cyclists could spend the night. There was a water hydrant and I drank deeply. I limped my water logged body over to a bench and laid down on top of it while I waited for everyone to meet me there.

I was so happy to see Brianne, the boys, and my parents. I walked across the street back out into the sun to join them in the camper van. My father was on the phone with Todd who had offered his place up in the mountains of Colorado for us to stay at for a couple of days while we passed through. I had met him at a meeting the month before we left. I had brought up our adventure and he lit up with excitement. He too had heard of the TransAmerican Trail and was a fan. He was just as excited about our trip as I was and wanted to help out. I updated him on our progress and then had a snack while we discussed where we would be spending the night. Brianne wanted to go to the geographic center of the Unites States around Lebanon and so we packed up my bike and all headed north. The heat did not let up and the SUV began to climb into the upper threshold of its operating temperature. We had to turn the air conditioning off and open the windows. This only kept the heat just under the red though and we both worried about what towing Isosceles in this heat was doing to the cooling system. We still had a great deal of miles to go before getting up into the cooler elevations of the Rockies and who knew what climbing them would do to the vehicle. We reached Russel and found a place where we could spend the night. We checked in, dropped the trailer, and said good night to my parents before heading north again for another hour and a half.

The center of the US was really neat. They had built a tiny church there and a decent picnic area. The boys ran around the site and I took pictures of them. While I was capturing the sign I noticed a strange artifact at the base of it. It was something made of clay in a plastic bag. I inspected it further picking it up and removing it from the bag. It was a clay fired red devil claw of some sorts. I was weirded out by it and put it back where I found it. Another car pulled up and a gentleman got out and started setting up some equipment. He must have been looking for the exact center as he kept moving a tripod with a device on top around until he seemed satisfied. He then took some pictures while we had our dinner at the picnic benches. Brianne began teasing me about the devil claw and I got even more weirded out. The guy left and another car pulled up with two younger people. They set to checking out the place as we packed up. The road that took us out ran back into what looked like forever. We headed down that road and then back toward Russel. There was a storm on the way and it rolled over the beautiful country side. Steep rolling hills ran parallel to the road pushing up the surrounding rocky terrain. I was glad we had gone out there and soon we were back at camp where sleep came easy enough and the night was comfortable.

We took a half rest day the following morning. Brianne and the boys slept in while I had coffee with my parents, watching the sun rise. The RV park was on the edge of town just off the freeway. We were parked on the outskirts of the lot and had an uninterrupted view of the plains as they ran off into the distance further than any of us could see. The weather had cooled just a bit overnight after the storm had passed through and we were comfortable. My mother soon put breakfast on and I awoke the rest of my family to come join us. The boys enjoyed having me there and the break was needed.

Brianne and I did laundry as the boys played on the playground next to the office where we had checked in. My mother watched them and my father stayed back at the camper to relax. My legs appreciated the rest but the day promised to be really hot later and I had missed the cooler time to ride. I began to rush our departure as the temperatures rose. We packed up and headed down south again to pick up the trail. There was a rest stop in Alexander just down the road from Rush Center and this was the best starting point for us to pull off to unload my bike. I lathered up on sunscreen while the boys used the restroom. It was already 100 degrees out and there were a couple of tents set up next to the restroom where some riders had decided their day had come to an end. There was a Southern wind now at about 17 miles per hour accompanied by some heavy gusts. You would think I would have been put off by this as it was not a tailwind but it made the heat a bit more tolerable. The ride was slow going into this cross wind. My bike computer told me the pavement heat had gotten up to 112 degrees. The pavement gets really hot out in the middle of no where. I made it through the first town on the route without much trouble and then the 20 miles into the next one with a little less energy for the pedals. The dryer climate of the area made me feel better than the humid parts of the country I had passed through but I had to down copious amounts of water to stay hydrated. My water had become super hot too and was not much of a comfort. It reminded my of how hot the water bottles used to get in Iraq during the day. When you knew you had to drink it to survive but there was no joy or refreshment in the process. I forced it down now too and had an egg salad sandwich at a gas station once I came across one. I bought a cheese Danish too but the heat robbed me of my appetite and so I tucked it away in my handlebar bag for later. My family met me another 16 miles down the road in the next town and we enjoyed some ice cream in the shade. I was really moving slowly now and was not looking forward to the last leg of the day but picked myself up to get it over with. After that there were only 16 more miles to push through on the way to Dighton. I could see the city limits around ten miles out as there was nothing but flat plains between us. I had to use the restroom and so I stopped at some dirt road that intersected the paved one I was on. I looked around in every direction to see if the coast was clear. Surprise, it was! There were no trees or rocks to block the view of any passer by but when nature calls you listen.

The wind became so strong at this point that it caught my helmet like a sail which I then used as a kite to pull me along at 8 miles per hour. I drifted into thoughts of what I would do when I arrived back home and then back into the effort of pedaling into such a hot wind. It was a long hard push but I made it. I had a hard time finding the city park once I arrived in Dighton as it was tucked away down one of their many side streets. It was covered in shade trees though and had a pool and a pavilion. Conor had burnt his hand on the playground equipment and showed me his blisters. We gathered in the pavilion to enjoy some fresh fruit and cold soda as we waited for the sun to start to set bringing back cooler temperatures. Brianna and Noah arrived and we enjoyed their company as we finished our dinner. Brianne and my mother took the boys swimming and I rested on a bench. The evening did bring cooler weather and the ceiling fan in Isosceles eased us through the warm night with a cross breeze. The next day we would be in mountain time and the day after that would put us well into Eastern Colorado.

When I awoke it was still very dark. Brianna and Noah were not stirring yet and I quietly used the hydrant by their tents to fill my water and wash up for the day without waking them. There was another bike off a ways in the park near the pool. I must have missed them coming in last night and never did get the chance to meet them. I took off down the side streets zig zagging my way back to the main road. Once I left town the wind picked up in my favor this time and it was not the oven of a tailwind that the late afternoons brought but a cool gentle shove out into the wilderness. I glided with the wind all morning. There was barely a moment that I was not going 19 miles per hour or more with the exception of the almost unnoticeable elevation changes on the way towards the mountains. The elevation was in a steady climb all day long but the change was not enough to bother me. I had at least two more days before any elevation changes worth noting. Soon I would be in the foothills of the Rocky Mountains and that was when things would get more difficult. I was so excited to cross over into Colorado the next morning and it gave me a great deal of energy. Now that I was going to be in mountain time I planned on getting up at 4AM instead of 5AM as it would feel the same and I could cover even more ground in the earlier part of the day. The sun had been slower to rise with me at this point in the mornings and the heat in Western Kansas was a dry one. I welcomed the dry heat as it was kinder to me but really looked forward to the cooler temperatures at the higher elevations that I would be encountering as I moved between mountain passes. The day was filled with excitement for the future as Kansas was winding down and one of my favorite states was just on the horizon.

I arrived before everyone else did in the border town of Tribune, thanks to the tailwind. I stopped in at a large gas station and had a cheese pizza along with a machine whipped mint chocolate chip shake. I watched people come and go as they stretched their legs no doubt on their way to Colorado too. I was just so happy to be there on the edge of the next leg of our adventure. When my family arrived they let me know they had passed Brianna and Noah about ten miles back and that they were planning on spending the night there as well. My parents were in the mood for hookups that night as we had boondocked the evening before and this was not as comfortable in the summer heat as having air conditioning. The clerk at the gas station had them drive up the road to catch a lady who drove us down the street to the grain elevators where my parents rented two parking spots for the night. The same woman then took us to a dirt lot tucked in between two empty buildings off the main road. Brianne and I looked at each other and said we would rather have no power and find the town park and pool instead. My parents came with us but planned on staying in the lot and so we got their money back for our spot. A truck driver from the grain elevator told us that there was a place tucked away back behind the pool where there was a large park. "That is where I would stay," he said. We headed over there and enjoyed the rest of the afternoon there in the shade as the children played. We took turns swimming in the pool and keeping the dogs company as the sun began to set. There were several teenagers who drove around our campers to check us out throughout the afternoon and so we decided that we would move camp to the place in front of the pool where the local sheriff had recommended we stay.

We found Brianna and Noah on our way to the grocery store to stock up on supplies. They had been using the internet at the public library and enjoying the cool air in there. The library was closing and we told them about the pool. We bought supplies to cook my parents an anniversary dinner and then went back to camp. The evening was a great success and we celebrated the many blessings we had been given in our lives. As the sun began to set we enjoyed Brianna and Noah's company too. As we were getting settled in for the night a very powerful front blew in and brought an epic tailwind with it. Brianna, Noah, and I joked about picking up camp and riding it through the night all the way into Colorado. I was only half joking as it would have been awesome to ride such a wind but it was late, dark, and my legs were still worn out from the riding earlier in the day. Brianna and Noah took shelter in the pool restrooms and we buttoned up Isosceles to ride out the storm.

Colorado

The breeze from the cold front had blown through the camper all night keeping the air inside chilled and blanket comfortable. The boys snuggled next to me as we slept. Predawn song birds awoke me about an hour before sunrise as they normally did at this point. It was a relief to ride in some chilly morning air for a change rather than the hotter and humid climate that I had come from. It felt like an eternity though to go the 15 miles to the Colorado border as I was very excited to cross over it. I made up a song about traveling to magic cookie mountain as I had jokingly dubbed it in the wake of the legalization of recreational marijuana. It was encouraging to see some of the states loosen up a bit on the subject especially since it has been found to assist with intractable epilepsy in some children. I was also excited to leave behind another state but would surly miss the lack of elevation changes in Kansas. Kansas by far had been the easiest state that I had ridden through to date if I let my mind forget about the endless summer heat and lack of shade. I eventually came across the colorful Colorado welcome sign that I had seen on so many YouTube videos of other fellow travelers. I was finally there.

The small towns of Eastern Colorado do not have very much in terms of services. The climate is semiarid with prickly pair cacti scattered here and there. I even came across a love seat complete with a scarecrow couple lounging in it and a deflated pumpkin at its side from the past fall I presumed. I had to stop and take a picture there and noticed a sticker from another cyclist who had been on their third cross country journey that summer. It was a robot with an antenna on its metallic head. I never crossed paths with him but did see several of his marks along the route after that. I also came across a small town with a diner and stopped in for some breakfast. The diner was decorated with vintage photographs and old items. It was dark inside and a few locals began to show up as I looked over the menu on the wall above the kitchen. Two gentleman sat down at a table by the checkout and then three more went into the back and sat down at the table near the stove. They helped themselves to the coffee and I followed suit. One of the old timers began to give the woman running the stove a hard time about her enthusiasm for working there that morning and you could tell it was a ritual with those two. I love usual places like that where a local population gathers to commune before their daily toils and you can tell this is their sense of being part of a community. The waitress/cook/manager took my order last as I was the outsider. The food was really good and the price was about as low as I have seen for breakfast at a diner. The crowd began to warm up to my presence as the food was served and the man who had given the woman a hard time turned around in his chair to include me in on the conversation of the day. It turned out he used to drive a long haul truck to the West Coast and back for many years. He knew the route I was taking and said he might just hop on his bike and join me. His table mate laughed, "You don't even own a bike!" You could tell that their was some longing for adventure in his jest though. By the time I had finished up and paid, everyone was saying goodbye to me like I belonged there. One of the gentleman in the back even said he would see me tomorrow morning. On the way out of town my cell phone started to ring. I let it go to voicemail as I did not feel like stopping to fish it out as I had just gotten back underway. You could go nowhere fast if you stopped to answer the phone or do any number of things throughout the day and so I just let it ring. Later I found out that I had missed yet another call from the healthcare exchange wanting to know why I had reported such a low expected income for the end of the year while I was working as a Director of IT Services. That was a battle I had been putting off until August and so I just let it go.

Later in the day I met up with my family in Eads. We had originally discussed spending the night there but the heat of the day was not as bad as had been expected and I wanted to push on to see if there were greener pastures than the rocky desert that I saw before me. That evening Brianna and Noah would tell me that they too had stopped in Eads to eat lunch at the restaurant next to the gas station. Their waitress had told them that any cyclist who was riding in the middle of the lane deserved to die. She was a firm believer in the roads being just for cars. We all laughed about it at dinner that night. My experience in Eads was much more pleasant. The gas station clerk had let me fill up my soda twice and I enjoyed some ice cream too. Brianne told me that a van had pulled out behind them from some lonesome dirt road around the love seat scarecrows and had followed them all the way into town before passing slowly by them to head back the way they had come. It freaked her out a bit but who knows maybe they had forgotten something back home. The next town over was Haswell and that is where we would spend the evening. My family went on ahead to set up camp and I began to pedal again.

Haswell was very small and I came across the small convenience store right as I came into town. I was thirsty and pulled in parking my bike off to the side of the building. There was another cyclist sitting on a chair by the door and staring off into the distance. His lips were cracked and he looked just beat down. I knew he was one of the racers from the looks of him and his lightly packed bike. I talked with him for a moment about how the race was going and told him how much I admired his ability to push himself so hard. I let him know of the other racers that I had passed on the way too before reaching for the door handle to the store to enter. "They closed an hour ago," the racer told me with no joy in his voice. Well, that is unfortunate I replied and bid him good luck on the rest of his travels. I set off through town then to look for my family.

Everyone was on the other edge of town in a green space with a pavilion. There was a hydrant for water too and by God it was some of the sweetest, coldest, and clearest water I drank so far on my journey. Brianne told me that the town was named Haswell because it had a well. Best well water I had ever had. There was also a playground for the kids and the nation's smallest jail house just down the street. My favorite though was the old cement block outhouse that had seen better days and the sign spray painted on it that warned to use it at your own risk. Brianna and Noah arrived a little later and we all had pasta together for dinner. It was wonderful to all spend time together and recount our last week as we ate. We all slept well that night.

The next morning started out in the moonlit sky of the full harvest moon. It shown reddish orange hanging low over the semiarid high plains on its descent to meet the morning sun. The air was cool and the ride through the barren landscape was surreal as I left camp to venture out. I moved through the dark for around an hour and then the sun began to break over the horizon. Day came upon me quickly and the sun shown bright gold lighting up the edges of the clouds above. The temperature began to rise and kept doing so all day long. I just rode and kept riding alone into the landscape surrounding me. I passed an abandoned wooden structure and followed the road from there around large bends that went on for miles. The terrain began to rise a little in the afternoon and I caught my first hazy glimpse of the Rocky Mountain Range as I crested a small hill. I did not know whether it was a mirage or the real deal until they slowly began to gain more focus to them over the next hour of riding. There were resting train cars on tracks that ran along side the road and the dormant cars stretched on for miles. I was climbing in and out of multiple hills now and reached Boon in the early afternoon where we met for lunch. Boon was also were Brianna and Noah would part ways with us on the journey as they were headed north from there to Colorado Springs and we would move up into the mountains through Pueblo and then Cañon City. I really had enjoyed their company as our paths had crossed many times along the trail heading up until that moment.

Lunch was quick as everyone was excited to get to Pueblo were we would have RV hookups and some much needed rest. We had planned on staying at Lake Pueblo State Park and it was along the route on the other side of town making it a great staging point for the next day as well. It was Father's Day and I had wanted some Mexican food. The last time I had been in Pueblo was many years ago on business and I remembered having some of the best sopapillas I had ever had.

After lunch I rode off and in a couple of miles popped my twentieth spoke. It was the final one that I had brought for that rim. I had 8 more that I bought in Missouri but they were in the camper miles ahead of me. You would think I would have put more in my panniers for the day but such is life. With no spare to replace it I rode on and just hoped for some better luck. Further down the way I came upon a weird place were they had erected a tall chain fence, covered it with green snow fence material, and put up video cameras all over the place to watch over some type of crops they were growing in there. I imagined it was a secret marijuana science project. I rode on into the outskirts of Pueblo where the road widened considerably, the traffic picked up, and the speed of the passing vehicles increased as well. The shoulder was wider there too but littered with debris. Brianne and my parents met me at a gas station just before the more congested part of the city. I picked up a roofing nail heading into the parking lot and experienced my first flat tire of the journey. Pueblo was the half way marker on the Trans-American Trail and I had made it there on my two original inner tubes. My rear cassette was so worn out at this point that the chain slipped every time I put too much gusto into a stroke of the pedals making for difficult riding up the new hilly terrain. My tires were also showing a large strip of the yellow warning material letting you know that they were bald, traction-less, and at the end of their lives. I had planned for this very moment months before hand and had all the parts needed for a full service stop once we made camp that evening. Brianne and the boys had gotten me a cherry icee to celebrate this great Father's Day halfway across the entire country from where our journey had begun. I felt loved.

The state park was awesome but super hot. Isosceles' air conditioning could not keep up with the heat and we all suffered for hours before the sun finally started to descend. I changed out my tires, rear wheel with the one I had built, chain, and rear cassette. I took my bicycle for a spin around camp and it rode just like it had on the first day of the journey! No more slipping chain for me as I got up to speed or while trying to ascend a grade. The bike was ready for the thousands of miles still ahead and I was enjoying the feeling of being half done with such an epic adventure.

Dinner at the restaurant was all right but they were pretty much anti-vegetarian. Brianne and I found some good choices though in a salad and cheese quesadilla. We enjoyed the meal in the end. At the campsite the kids played at the park in the dark by the light of the moon and I ate half a tub of ice cream that we had picked up at a Walmart on the way back. With the next day came the ascent into the mountains and I needed some extra calories for the work ahead.

The morning started out warm with some immediate climbing. My legs had forgotten how to climb steep grades while I was in the flats of Kansas and they ached. The mountains were just off into the distance now and I was in their foothills. The terrain was beautiful to behold and my eyes drank it all in. I met another one of the TransAm racers, this one from Italy, and we stopped to talk in the middle of the road swapping pictures and commenting on how wonderful this adventure had turned out to be. He was just about halfway done with his race and had stopped everywhere along the way to experience the world around him. He was out their for the fun of it and could not care less about his placement at the end. We wished each other well and I went down a long stretch of road that flattened out for a moment at a creek. A sheriff was out there investigating a car that had jumped off the bridge and into the dry creek bed below. It was lying on its hood and I could not see how the passenger could have survived the horrific looking accident. The sheriff gave me a look that said be careful out there and went back to his work, so did I.

I ran across another rider coming eastbound and stopped to chat with him for half an hour. He was out on a week long journey trying out his new touring bike. He had really invested much time and resources into his bicycle and we admired it together as I applied more sunscreen and ate an orange. I wished him well and told him I really had to get on my way if I was going to get very far for the day. He let me know that there was a restful long downhill stretch after the steep grade up ahead and I thanked him for the good news.

The grade was very steep indeed and it took a lot out of me to climb it. It was not as bad as the Appalachians but the difference between it and the grades from over the last week was stark. My speed turned quickly into a crawl as I worked hard to climb. My heart picked up to a steady drum beat to match the forced labor and I felt a little weak in the legs. There was a couple tending to their property down the ridge to my right. The man was working on the fence while the woman washed their child in a plastic water trough. I would love to homestead like them someday and admired their choice to live apart from the modern social structure that most of us have subscribed to.

After a very long haul I finally crested the ridge and it crossed over to a small town where I searched out the local library to fill my water bottles. I found the library empty but unlocked. I poked around the building until I found a set of stairs that led to the basement where the bathrooms were located. I tested the faucet water in the men's room. The water tasted harsh like chemicals and minerals. I passed. It was unfortunate too because I was very low on water but getting sick accomplished nothing. I left town and was happy to see the road did indeed tend downward after that for a very long stretch. I added some electrolyte tablets to the last of my water making it last longer. I ran completely out a few miles later. I did come across a Super 8 Motel and the manager was more than happy to let me fill up on ice and water there. I thanked him and sat outside recovering from the heat while I spoke with Brianne on the phone for a spell before getting back on the bike and out into the sun again. I had my second flat tire of the trip a block from the Motel. I had picked up a thin metal wire that worked itself right through my brand new puncture resistant tires and into the soft rubber inner tube wall beneath. I lost my spare inner tube while I was filling it with my small hand pump. The force of my pumping cracked the rubber valve stem and then I was stuck. I had no way of fixing the bike at this point and so I called Brianne to save me.

We all eventually made it to Cañon City which turned out to be larger than I had remembered it on my business trips out there. The day turned very hot and our SUV began overheating again. We planned on spending the night at Todd's cabin up in the higher elevations but the vehicle could not make the climb in the heat of the day. At one point it buried the temperature needle in the red and automatically shut down to save itself from blowing a gasket. We went back into the city to wait out the heat after that. There was the worlds tallest suspension bridge to see and a Walmart to stock up at too. The boys loved the golf cart ride from the RV parking lot to the entrance of the bridge and the old steam engine that they had staged outside was tops with them as well. After a little exploring we all headed down into the downtown area to shop for food and rest. The shade trees were all staked out by panhandlers. I saw two of them go at it as it appeared that one had encroached upon the other's territory. Their lives looked difficult and the hot sun did not seam to make them any better. The one who lost the fight over the prime corner retreated with his dog back to an old RV. He sat there for a long time just looking forward before settling down and reading a book. The other started pan handling and the afternoon went on in the heat. When we grew restless we moved on to the city park where it was heavily shaded and much cooler. There was a bathroom that smelled of fresh smoked weed and a fountain to fill our water bottles. We got folding chairs out and chatted for several hours. The boys played in the grass at our feet. I texted Todd to let him know of our overheating troubles and he was so kind as to offer to pay for us to sit in a hotel while we waited. I could not take him up on it as it was too much but I appreciated it just the same. He spoke with a meteorologist friend back in Omaha and told us we really needed to be out of Cañon City that evening as a large storm front was moving in and the heat would be even worse the next day. So we gave it another shot once the temperature had fallen to 88 degrees.

I really thought we would make it that time but it was more of the same. In fact we had to stop at the exact same point as the last time we had attempted the climb in the 100 degree heat. We made the call then and there to abandon the cabin and I hopped out to assemble my bicycle for the ride ahead. So I took to pedaling up the steeper grades in the heat as the sun started to set and my family waited for the SUV to cool down before moving ahead. We had dumped the freshwater tank and moved about 100 pounds of dry goods over to the camper van before I left to give them more of a chance to make forward progress. They drove past me in about 20 minutes and then I was alone again out on rural highway 9 heading north.

The sun was almost gone now and I soon took out my lights in order to see and be seen if a vehicle came up from behind. There was a dry creek bed to my right and small homesteads dotting the landscape here and there. I even came across a yurt at one point. The yurt was right on the creek bed and I wondered just how safe it would be in a storm. That is about the time I started to hear the thunder and feel the temperature drop about 15 degrees. There was a storm moving in and it looked ominous. The clouds had a heavy swirl to them and a truck heading south stopped to warn me of the quarter sized hail heading my way. There was also a tornado to the East and they thought I should seek shelter. They drove off and I thought it would have been appreciated if they had offered to take me up the road to Guffey where I was headed. I imagine they were not thrilled to be out in the weather either though. It became darker and darker. I pedaled hard up the grade and could not see myself making it in time. I knew I would need to find shelter if the hail came and I looked around for such places to crawl into if it came to it. Just when I had about three miles left to go and the wind started to really bare down on me my parents drove past and circled back to pick me up. I did not want to go at first but common sense prevailed and I rode with them into Guffey. We pulled into town behind the Bull Moose Restaurant and Bar where the man who ran the place said we could spend the night. Brianne told me that he was very kind and made sure they were all set before heading home for the evening. I got into the warm camper just as it began to rain and then hail. The hail was quarter sized. I matched the ice balls to a quarter for a photo just in case we needed to make an insurance claim later on. We had our dinner under the roar the ice made on the camper's roof top. It was cold out that evening and we used the propane heater to add some warmth. I was thankful for the ride into Guffey from my parents and the kindness of the bar keep. A chilly night was a blessing compared to what the last several weeks had been like. We finally had made it into the elevation that I had been chasing for so long. I knew it would be my kind of riding weather from there on.

The next day was just beautiful. I woke up right as the sun started to rise over the mountains that surrounded Guffey. The air was crisp and I put on my gloves and cap before heading out. Guffey was a cool town. I wish I had spent more time there but the road called and so I left. There were great climbs all morning into scenic views of mountains, treeless rises, and snow topped peaks. The scene just took my breath away both metaphorically and physically. I felt the air begin to thin as I ascended working my legs constantly through the slow climbs. The rises were not as steep as the Appalachian Mountains had been but they were at a higher elevation and that added to their difficulty. I was alone in the quiet wilderness.

Brianne told me later in the day that the SUV had no trouble pulling the camper to the top of each rise in the cool of the morning air and that made me glad as I had been worried about its ability to make it though the mountain passes. We decided to get the coolant serviced in Frisco when we stopped to see my Aunt Kathy and Uncle Don there.

The sun proved to be much stronger up at this elevation than it had been down below on the high plains. I became a little burned as the cool air fooled me into feeling fine without sun screen. The road was filled with multitudes of ground squirrels who darted across here and there. I was too slow to disturb them and so we all made use of the road together. I had to dodge a few of them on occasion but no close calls thank goodness. There were just so many of them. I passed by bison and pedaled in and out of rises as I continued my climb to the Southern most park in Colorado. There are three parks, high valleys, surrounded by mountains as you head north. I was both energized and excited to arrive in Hartsel about three hours later.

I pulled into town from the South and then crossed onto the main street stopping in front of the cafe. I took a seat on one of the old wooden benches just outside to wait for Brianne and the boys. They had gone on ahead to secure a place to stay and were backtracking to meet me there. My parents went on to Frisco to spend another day with Kathy and Don so it would just be us from here to there. We passed through Hartsel the year before on our camping trip through the Rockies and I was happy to have returned. Brianne pulled into a parking spot off the highway and we embraced with a smile. I helped her get the boys out of the SUV and we walked into the cafe to sit down. It was an older cafe with mostly wooden walls and tables. I noticed the outlet near our table and asked the waitress if I could plug my phone in. "Sure you can, would you like some coffee?" I did want some coffee and we looked at the menus as she brought some out. Two Great Divide racers also stopped in and we had some fun talking with them about their journeys.

They were part of the race across the Great Divide from The Northern border of the country to the Southern one. It is an extreme off road adventure that takes the rider up steep mountain pass after mountain pass and through multiple climates. One of the men gave me a short back rub and then sat down to enjoy some steak and eggs. His companion rider was a bit saddened by the fact that they had gotten behind the lead racers. "I think we are just touring the Great Divide at this point," he sighed. I admired them both either way. Their travels took them into parts of the American wilderness without any services at all. They had specialized bikes built with huge knobby tires and packed everything they needed across their handle bars and in a bag that jutted out from the seat at an upward angle. The TransAmerican racers had a very light version of this configuration on a road bike. We all enjoyed mountains of good food and could not have asked for better company. I kissed Brianne and the boys good bye and started to head out for the last part of the day. We were headed to South Park from there where Brianne had stationed Isosceles by a creek in a gravel RV park. Another TransAmerican cyclist pulled in as I was leaving and I stopped to chat with him for a moment. His name was also Dan and he was heading westbound as well. I wished him safe travels and hopped onto the saddle once more.

The rest of the ride to South Park went well. It was slow going but so beautiful I did not care about the grades. My legs were also getting used to them now. There were mountain streams and even more peaks to take in as I went. I turned down one road by a stream and waved at Brianne and the boys as they explored the local spot. Later Brianne honked at me as she passed by. There was a stone works along the way with bronze figures standing on top of a long stone wall. I imagined them protecting their fortress. Eventually, I turned into South Park and worked my way through heavier traffic than I had seen for days. I missed the RV park as it was hidden from my view and had to call Brianne several times to make my way to her. The park was down a long gravel hill and you could hear the rush of the rapids as they crashed into the river rocks. I went inside and took a nap while everyone watched a movie. Later we went into town and explored the shops and coffee house. The boys and I picked out a strawberry cake to take back with us for later and then we headed to the camper for the evening. I cooked mashed potatoes, corn, and green beans for dinner and we ate outside in the fresh air. A storm looked like it was moving in and so we picked up our things to head indoors. There was a laundry and shower trailer too which we made use of as it became dark. It was good to be clean again and we slept well in the mountain air.

In the morning I helped Brianne and the boys pack up the RV before I headed out. She had a long climb to the top of Hoosier Pass and I wanted to make sure that she got out of the camp site as early as possible to drive in the cooler temperatures. The ride started off on a grade as I left town and ventured forth to Alma. There was a bicycle path between the two towns and the sign that signified the start of it was a little misleading. I almost followed it up into a neighborhood on the edge of town. I stopped just before it turned sharply up and thought about where I was going before making the mistake of climbing that grade just to have to turn around and back track to the point I was at again. I made the right decision and followed the road. The trail started as the shoulder and then separated from the road and onto its own path which ran up and down over pavement in need of repairs in some areas. The road would have been smoother and easier to travel on but being out of the traffic as the altitude changes sucked the breath from me was also a good way to travel this morning. It took me so long to cover the small distance between there and Alma that Brianne called worried about the delay. She had gotten used to me moving with a purpose over the last several weeks and now I was inching my way forward. My breath was labored and I was thankful that I was in better shape than I was when I started the journey in Yorktown. At some point I went down a hill for a ways before returning to a smaller grade on the way into Alma. Everything was so beautiful up there.

I rode up to the Alma Coffee House that Don had recommended to me on the phone the day before. That was where Brianne and the boys were waiting for me. They had ordered me a breakfast burrito and I got a 16 ounce Mocha too. It was so good and I needed the nourishment for the ascent ahead. The burrito had egg, pico de gallo, and fried potato. This was my favorite breakfast burrito combination. I make them at home from time to time and they just hit the spot chasing away the hunger and springing the tastebuds into life. The coffee was perfect and the shop had an alpine lodge feel to it. Brianne and the boys left and I lingered on for a bit more. I took a photo of myself sitting there alone with my coffee. I looked tired and a little older than I liked to think of myself. I had begun to get white hairs in my beard the year before and they were gaining on their red and brown counterparts across my cheeks and under the chin. I was 36 now and my youth was getting away from me. Still young by most men's standards but not fresh anymore. I had arthritis in my neck and lower back from my time in the military and now white hairs coming in. At least I had this great adventure to fill my spirit with the awesome world that our creator had made for us. So I sat there in the warmth of the lodge on the edge of the pass to summit the highest elevation on the entire journey, Hoosier Pass.

At some point I saddled up and started the last five mile climb to the top of the pass. The pass was 11,542 feet above sea level. The first mile was easy but the grade quickly became steeper. I kept pedaling. The miles went on at a crawl and took forever at that point. The air became very difficult to find the oxygen I needed to be able to push my legs so hard. I was sucking in the air and quickly exhaling it with the sound of my heart pounding in my head. The snow capped mountain peaks that had been far off into the hazy distance were now right in front if me. I could smell the ice in the air. Had I been out there all alone I might have been tempted to park the bike and hike to the top of one of them just to know that I had but there was family waiting for me at the top of the pass. After a long time I began to hear what I thought were moose or elk calling out in the woods. It soon became clear though that it was Brianne, the boys, my parents, aunt, and uncle cheering me on! I passed a woman heading down the other side toward the South and she smiled at me as she flew by. She was racing the TransAmerica too but had been hit by a car in Oregon breaking some bones. She was determined to go as far as her body would allow her not giving in to defeat easily. What a strong person. I was so blessed to be in the presence of such strong people all along the way.

I was elated to have reached the highest point on the TransAmerican Trail! All of the future climbs should be easier in comparison to this one. It was great to see my aunt and uncle again too as we only get to see each other once a year around the holidays. We all took several pictures at the sign marking the pass and then I headed down to Breckenridge over the other side.

The descent quickly took me up to speeds of 42 miles per hour and I loved it. There were some hairpin turns but they were fun! I had new tires on and they gripped the road nicely as I leaned hard into the switchbacks. I was careful not to arc out into oncoming traffic on the release of the turns and loved the wild freedom of the coast. There was a bubbling stream to my right and the air smelled of pine and wind. I had planned on stopping at the Cannabis Club of Breckenridge across from the crepe place in the upstairs of the yellow building on main street. I had seen it there before on business and was in a mood for exploration. I hit the brakes as I cruised into town and then stopped at the lights. I waited with two other cyclists and then proceeded cautiously as the lights turned green again. The cars only half looked out for me and I made sure to fully look out for them. I came upon the shop only to find that the local voters had decided that it did not belong on main street anymore and had forced it to move elsewhere. I was a little saddened by this but there was still a Starbucks down the road to nurse these wounds. I walked my bicycle to the crosswalk and headed across. My helmet fell off the back of my rear rack where I had rested it and a pedestrian picked it up and handed it to me. I was grateful for their kindness and thanked him.

I Like to Ride

The barista in the Starbucks was super friendly and I felt at home there as I had the many other times I came there before. The mocha was dark and rich just how I remembered it and I sipped it while I waited for my family to get parked and meet me on main street near the crepe place where we were to have lunch. The crepe place in Breckenridge was a bit of a pricy place to grab a bite to eat but it is super cool and I love their killer selection. It is a tiny little cart on main street with three to four people crammed in there cooking crepes all day long. I like to get a sweet and then a savory crepe to satisfy my craving. My family soon caught up with me and we had lunch behind the stand. The sun felt warm on my face as we ate and I began to recount the journey so far for Kathy and Don. My uncle announced that he had brought his bicycle up with him and wanted to ride with me down the path to Frisco. I warned him that I was going to find the cannabis shop before leaving town which he did not mind. We walked back with everyone to the lift parking lot. Don got his bike down from the rack on their SUV and then we pushed off down the side streets.

The cannabis shops of Breckenridge were crammed together in one strip mall tucked deep away from the main parts of town. We stopped in and the aroma immediately punched our nostrils. A laid back bouncer checked our drivers licenses and then let us proceed into the purchase area with a long glass counter filled with any and every thing you could dream of infusing with the plant. Their were cookies, soda, candy, chocolate, and the smokable kind too. I bought a sleeve of cookies and my uncle chatted with the young woman behind the counter about the CBD oil and how it was used to treat epilepsy. Brianne and I knew of its health benefits for people with seizure disorders from our research on our son Aaron's Ohtahara Syndrome. It works like a miracle for some and does little for others. We know some families who have children with full seizure control due to the plant and that is why I will always feel that it should be a legal option for them. Recreationally, I could not care less but there I was on a mission to explore and so I partook. From there my uncle took me to the Breckenridge Distillery where I bought a bottle of bourbon. It came at a hefty price but I planned on sending it home to savor upon my return. After that we hit the Broken Compass for a pint of coconut oatmeal stout before making our decent.

The bike path to Frisco was great and downhill most of the way. It felt so good to be back in the higher elevation of the mountains where the lack of oxygen gave one a peaceful euphoric feeling as long as they were coasting or at rest. I slept like the dead that night.

We spent the next two days catching up with Kathy and Don. They have a home in Frisco and were very kind to have us all there at the same time. I spent the mornings walking Gabriel down to the city park and then across to the main street where I backtracked to the house. The kids enjoyed the structure of being in a stationary home for the moment and the break from constant pedaling was very welcomed.

In the afternoon Don and Kathy rented a boat at the marina on Lake Dillon and we cruised around relaxing in style. Conor and Aaron got to drive the boat sitting on Don's lap and Conor will tell you to this day that this was the best part of the trip for him. Later in the evening we met up with Brianna, Noah, and their family. We all had cake and ice cream at the park under the pavilion. It was outstanding to catch up with our friends and to meet their awesome family. Brianna had decided to venture forth again from Pueblo but Noah's adventure had come to an end. We joked with him that he would change his mind but his desire was to see his sister safely through to Colorado Springs which he had dutifully fulfilled. We let Brianna know she could call Brianne if she needed assistance from there on but she would not have the need. After dinner we all hugged goodbye and walked back to the house to sleep.

The next day Don and I rode all around town from repair shop to dealerships to see if the coolant could be serviced on the SUV before we left in the morning the next day. No one was available but a mechanic that just so happened to be good friends with Dan, who I had met in Hartsel, agreed to take a quick look offering some sound advice. He felt that the primary fan was inactive and this was the root cause of our issue. We thanked him and went to a parts store to get some fuses and relays to try out. None of them fixed the fan. The mechanic told us we should be fine though on the secondary fan as long as we did not let it redline anymore. Brianne and I decided the repair could wait for a bigger city where there would be a dealership who could assist us in the 24 hour period we would have to fix the SUV before moving on down the road again.

We all had a final dinner together that night. Brianne and I cleaned out Isosceles and packed her up for the final half of the journey. We went to bed excited to move forward and sad to leave such a wonderful place. My father headed back to Omaha from there and my mother would catch up with us a day or two down the road.

The morning came quickly and I awoke just as the sun was starting to rise. I checked Google Maps one last time before heading down the path that led to the park behind the homes along the stream. At the park I turned out onto the main street and then stopped at the red light to wait for my turn arrow. A sheriff was sitting off to the side of the road waiting for someone to come by too quickly and I waved at him as the light changed. I curved left onto the busier road that went through the new business district. I took a right onto the dam road right before the interstate and was on the dam just as the sun crested the mountains with its glorious rays of golden light. I moved across looking out over the water and then exited near some condos on the Silverthorne side. From there I got onto another busy road and cruised down the hill to meet back up with my route out of town.

It was really all down hill from there to Kremmling. Highway 6 became 9 and I rode around 22 miles per hour until I hit the end of the paved surface. There had been some construction on 9 out there for at least a year before and the road was just mud, sand, loose gravel, and dirt. The going was rough for around seven miles. I had several things bounce off the bike and made multiple stops to pick them up. At one point the gravel was so soft and deep that I almost spilled the bike but luckily stayed upright and safe. Kremmling was not far down the road from the start of the pavement at the end of the construction and I visited the gas station on the edge of town. Brianne, the boys, and I had stopped there the last summer to get a refreshing lime aid and licorice twists.

I waited there now for Brianne and enjoyed some soda. Continental divide racers came and went along with many other travelers. I was happy to see my family once they arrived. We ate a light lunch in the SUV by the grass near the gas station sign while the sprinklers spritzed the vehicle. After an hour I geared back up and was off again to finish the day out.

Later down the road a van started to honk at me and pulled off onto the shoulder to say something to me. I was a little leery of being hailed in such a fashion and was on guard as I pulled up next to them. It turned out to be Brianna, Noah, and family! They were off scouting the route ahead for Brianna before taking her back to the Pueblo area. I was so glad to get the chance to see them one last time and can still see Brianna waving to me. I was just three miles from Hot Sulfur Springs when they took off and it was an enjoyably easy ride in.

Brianne and the boys had found some public land for us to camp in and I quickly found it crossing the old bridge over the river that went through town. The land was in a flood plain and was partially submerged with water in some parts. The mosquitos were thick there and we were camped across a small pool of water. It was hot out in the sun and we tried to cool ourselves in the shade while the last part of the day turned into dusk. Conor worked on a maze booklet and Aaron napped along with Brianne. The air became cool once the sun set and then cold as the night took hold. The next evening was to be our last in Colorado. From there it would be on to Wyoming.

It was cold out when I left the next morning. The sun was just starting to rise above the surrounding mountains and I shivered a bit as I pedaled over the water and up the hill to the main road. I got about half a mile just on the edge of town before realizing that I had forgotten my water bottles. There was no way I was going to go anywhere without water and so I turned around and coasted all the way back down to the camp site. I cursed a little as I picked them up where I had left them on the hood of the SUV and I began to climb back through town once more. There were few shops or restaurants left on the main street and I could only assume that this hot spring destination had lost some of its allure over the years.

Once out of town I came across a woman jogging out in the cold. Large puffs of breath jetted out from her mouth like a steam engine running along its tracks. I wished her a good day as I rode past and she shouted out, "Enjoy your ride!" I knew that I would once I warmed up a little bit more. The road took me out into vast mountainous wilderness and by scattered homesteads. There was a giant mountain to my left at one point blocking all but the strongest rays of sunlight and I passed by into the full sun on the other side. From there I turned left down an even smaller road that started to climb. An airport shuttle passed by me scurrying to drop off or pick up a landowner out there somewhere. There were a few short down hill coasts that sent ice cold air into my helmet freezing my temples and causing my head to sting. My light gloves did little to protect my fingers which were wrapped around the handle-bars but I was glad to have them. At some point I rode into the Arapaho National Forest and began to climb again. The scenery was strikingly beautiful with a river that snaked through the mountains flanking me on both sides. I rode like the river winding here and there but against the current. The cool air did not warm until I reached the steepest grade on the way to summit Willow Creek Pass. I passed by primitive camp sites and stopped in an open area near the river for an orange and granola bar break. I rested with my face turned toward the sun for warmth and took my jacket off to air out the moisture built up from my perspiration. The mosquitos began to bite and I sprayed down with DEET. They swarmed off to find some other hapless wanderer who had forgotten their DEET that morning.

After I had eaten and rested I began the summit. It was a long haul but not as terrible as Hoosier or some of the Appalachian climbs I had made. I was both tired and happy when I reached the top of the pass where the continent divided again. I stopped to rest and take some pictures. Brianne and the boys met me at the top just before I was about to descend into the North Park. We had a filling meal and a rest before I headed out again.

The way down the other side of the pass was awesome. All the climbing I had done earlier in the day was now paying off in spades as I only had to pedal every now and again to go a little up before another big down. Of course I popped a spoke about 10 miles down the descent but I was so good at fixing those. The time spent on the side of the rode paid off too as I got to meet Rick who was also westbound. He had spoken with Brianne in Sulphur Hot Springs after I left that morning and now we got to talk for a spell too. He was taking his time and enjoying the days. I would have probably taken some more time too if the boys did not have school to return to in mid August. Who knows though as I also liked to cover a good amount of ground every day too.

After Rick and I parted ways the wind turned into a gusty head and cross wind. My pace slowed down to a crawl and I had to really work for the last half of the day. There was a wild fire burning off in the distance that I continued to ride closer to. Its smoke rose and spread out across the park. I was out in the vast open flat lands being assaulted by wind and sand. It grew warmer out again and by the time I rolled into Walden I was covered in sand. It had especially collected around my eyebrows and I felt both exhausted and dirty. My lungs were heavy from wrestling my breath in the wind and from sucking in the fine sand. I was spent.

I met Brianne and the boys at the rest stop just as I came into town. Conor had been talking to a woman there who was traveling alone in her RV. She had listened to him speak of the different viruses and bacteria he had been learning about. She listened on with great attention as he spoke of school, family, and his travels. They went back and forth as I put my head down on the picnic table in the shade to rest. Conor was glad to have a fresh audience and volunteered to watch her dogs while she used the restroom. When she returned she said she needed to move on and went to her camper. Before she left though she returned told Conor that she felt like she needed to give him a gift and all she could find was a dollar bill. Conor told her that he would spend it to feed his family and she began to cry a little as she turned to leave. It was a touching moment that I will cherish.

We waited there until my mother rejoined us. She was ready to finish the journey now and my father was back in Omaha safe and sound looking after their home. I really wish he had come with us to explore the wilds of this last half of America. We were together again and I rode up a small hill into town following my family in search of the park where we had arranged to spend the night.

The park was really a beautiful green space with modern bathrooms and a water hydrant. The fire fighters from the Forest Service were encamped around the school across the street. We watched helicopters coming and going throughout the evening dropping bags of fire retardant off in the distance as we ate dinner, played at the park, and then crashed in our beds. The air began to cool quickly as the sun went down and then became cold but not as frigid as the night before. This was our last overnight in Colorado. I wanted to see what came next but was so sad to leave the state I had looked forward to riding thorough the most. I could say then that I had conquered the Appalachians, Ozarks, and the Rockies.

Wyoming

Conor, my mother, and I had French toast for breakfast in her camper van. It hit the spot to have a big breakfast before heading out for the day. The morning was cold but not as cold as yesterday and Conor snuggled in a sleeping bag next to me as we ate. Brianne and Aaron slept in and I stopped in to kiss them both good bye as I left.

The riding was all downhill from Walden with a slight breeze at my back. I made it to the Wyoming border in no time flat. My top speed coming out of North Park was 51.2 miles per hour, my fastest yet. I would have been afraid to travel at such a speed the months before now but the bike felt like an extension of my body at this point and I was perfectly at ease hanging down low over the handlebars, face near the front wheel, and feeling the whirl of wind coming at me. The black Alpine flags on their long poles whipped in the wind on both sides of the road as I tore into Wyoming and said goodbye to Colorado. I was excited to see the Grand Tetons for the first time in my life but would miss the Rockies. The rest of the day was not so easy as I turned into the wind and had some climbs to accompany the flats and downs. There was no joy in the downs as the wind pushed back at me sucking all of the momentum right out of me. I did meet several eastbound cyclists along the way though and stopped to chat. One was Roberto from Milan Italy. He wanted to know where to sleep and find water up ahead. There was a slight language barrier but we understood each other well enough to laugh about the thin air of the passes and to enjoy each other's company. With a final ciao we were both on our way again in opposite directions. I popped a spoke about eight miles from Saratoga were we were to meet up but let it ride as I tended to do those days.

Saratoga was a larger town and it had a tourist destination feel to it as I passed through. The traffic picked up and I crossed paths with many cyclists who had stopped for burgers, ice cream, and many other comforts before heading out into the wild unknowns again. I had to ride all the way through town and out the other side to find Saratoga Lake where Brianne and my mother had set up camp. There was a really nasty ruin of what had once been a road that wound its way for a mile out to the lake and I took care not to pop another spoke while traversing it. The lake was pretty much void of people and we parked at the RV sites. There was power to hook up to but a sign warned us not to partake of the well water lest we succumb to heavy metal afflictions. As much as that sounded just awesome we skipped it. We settled in and then I went with my mother to dump her blackwater tank along with our cassette tank out at the sewage treatment plant. It had one of those fancy credit card accepting locks on it that gave you a minute or so to drain your tank as fast as you possibly could before it locked up on you again. It was a quick and dirty job but I got it done. From there we all went into town to spend a few hours at the public library, yes I washed my hands with soap. My mother worked on reading with the children while Brianne updated her blog and paid our bills. I hung out with Gabriel in the parking lot. As we sat in the back of the SUV enjoying the artificial breeze of a battery operated fan a pair of deer casually walked by and into a back yard across the way from us. Gabriel had no idea they were even there and I watched them poke around a bit before they headed off.

From the library we hit the hot springs which were really damn hot. We started in the river which was equally as cold as the springs were hot. We channeled the spring water into a pool and enjoyed the stinky sulfur infused mix for a good long while before venturing over to the really hot pools. These pools were not safe for the boys and so they showered and I tested them out. It took me at least fifteen minutes to get past my calves and into a sitting position. I could barely feel anything from the water level down and this was superbly relaxing. When I stepped out of the pool a couple pointed out that I was red as a lobster from my chest down. I showered before meeting back up with my family at the vehicles. We went shopping before heading back to camp and found that most of the locals used four wheelers to get around town. It was a unique place to visit and I recommend it if you are ever in those parts. We fought the mosquitos at dinner and all settled in early for the night.

Brianne made cinnamon oatmeal for breakfast accompanied by a latte she had mixed up for me. We had slept well with the hookups and the heat pump made the cool night just perfect. If I had not been so driven to complete the adventure I could have easily slept in on occasions like this and maybe even lingered a few more days there in the hot springs. It was time to move on though just as it had been almost every morning since we had left Yorktown.

The mosquitos were really thick and I hurried to get on the road as I fumbled with my bike to get the tires inflated to the proper riding pressure. The brakes also needed to be adjusted so they would not rub the rims. The road out of Saratoga Lake was so terrible that the sand shoulder offered a better surface for riding and so I took to it instead. I rode nonstop past the first gas station around 20 miles later and then merged onto I-80 interstate traffic on the way to Sinclair. It was a first for me, riding on the interstate. The shoulder was wide enough though, after the initial construction pushed me into riding mere feet away from the fast moving traffic. I came across a closed rest stop and saw a motorist using the wall outside of it. I would have used a bush or a tree but who was I to judge. I popped a spoke after a large semi-truck passed me shaking the pavement as it went, so I stopped to repair it. The air was hazy out there and I assumed it was from the wildfire that had been put out the night before. It could have also been in part from the oil refinery down the road too. I enjoyed the smooth grade of the interstate all the way to the Sinclair exit and stopped at the gas station to rest. On the way into the parking lot I came across three motorists who were posing in front of the Sinclair dinosaur. I offered to take their picture and they had a good time posing in all types of situations with the dino before thanking me and heading out. I took a few photos of my bicycle next to it and entered the store to get some soda and a snack. I found a slice of pumpkin pie to go along with a gigantic Mountain Dew. I enjoyed them both outside as I rested there for half an hour. A woman pulled up in a van and spent several minutes rounding up her children to go inside just to figure it was not worth the trouble at the front door and turned around to wrestle them all back into the vehicle. I felt bad for here as she was obviously stressed out from the situation and probably had wanted some refreshments. I chatted with some truck drivers about the wild fires, then decided to start riding again.

The road took me past the refinery and it reminded me of Kuwait. The town just down the street looked closed up since the main street was blocked off for construction. I rode around the barriers and made my way over the crazy post apocalyptic rode ahead. There were huge bulges and dips all over it. I wondered what had went down there. I have never seen such a thing before. I made a wrong turn on the way out of town and ended up on the on ramp to I-80 going east. I had no desire to do that, so I turned around and went back into town to see where I had gone wrong. There was a turnoff down a side street that I guess I should have been on the lookout for and I was once again on my way to Rawlins. The old route I was on was without traffic and I liked it. It did not take long to reach the city and I came across an eastbound cyclist once I hit the edge. I stopped to talk with him and found out he was from Europe and was living on the side of the road during his journey. He looked weathered and warned me of some questionable eating establishments in my future. He let me know that he would ride from dawn until dusk and then just slip off the side of the road when no one was looking to disperse camp there. I was sure to let him know to stop in and see Violet in Sebree.

Once in Rawlins I made straight for the McDonalds for an egg and cheese biscuit but my long wait in line turned out to be a bust. No biscuits after breakfast at this McDonalds either. Apparently I did not read the small print on their breakfast at any time of the day campaign. Although, this afforded me the opportunity to have a seven layer burrito with Brianne, my mother and the boys over at Taco Bell. We feasted on all sorts of bad for you but oh so yummy concoctions. I was sure to burn off the calories anyway. Lunch was great. I took the boys to the restroom over at the gas station next door and then applied sun screen out in the parking lot while Brianne and my mother loaded up the boys into the SUV. It was getting hot out down there in the lower elevations and I had some riding to do before the sun went down. I hit the road again, riding out of the biggest city I had been in for some time. I pushed on up and over another continental divide. This one was a long and drawn out grade that was easy to pedal up but went on forever. Then I was down the other side into a beautiful valley surrounded by red rocked peaks and big open sky. I got yelled at by a guy on a motorcycle as he passed and I waved at him not knowing what he had said. His return gesture told me that it was not positive whatever it had been. I rode on for what felt like an eternity from there down terrible shoulders with heavy traffic zooming by just to my left at a steady pace. At one point a wide load semi came really close to me and I decided that this road was not the safest for cycling. I had multiple encounters with wide load tractor trailer combinations on the journey thus far.

The closest was in Western Kansas where a trailer stacked to the heavens with hay passed another such loaded trailer while passing me. I could have touched the hay to my left without extending my arm more than a foot. This of course had all occurred as the truck passing me was going around 50 miles per hour. Brianna and Noah had reported getting stopped by a trucker out in those parts so he could ask them to warn all the other cyclists not to ride out there that time of year. It "just wasn't safe," he had said. They found some humor in his assumption that they would be able to spread the word for him even if they had wanted to. Another wide load trailer with construction equipment had forced me off the road in Virginia. There was a crew of construction workers on the other side of the road forcing him over into me and one of the workers laughed towards me, "He almost squished you!" That he did buddy, that he did. I had another near miss with a yellow pickup truck in the Appalachian Mountains when the driver crossed the center line and headed straight for me. I thought is was a joke at first but then I saw his texting thumbs tapping away at his phone and his face down without a care for what was in the road. I moved out of his way too. I had been blessed so far though and there was no reason to fear the traffic more than what was healthy at that point in the trip.

There were storms brewing in small cells all around me as I began to ride out into what appeared to be a vast salty flat basin. I did not know if I should be worried about them as I could see them moving about here and there but had no idea if our paths would ever meet. There were mountains dotting the landscape and one of the dark cells moved over one striking out with vicious flicks of lightning. The wind became just brutal as I intersected another storm front while traversing around one of the mountains. I had to change gears into one that I only reserved for the most steepest of grades just to move forward. This was one of the reasons I had come on this journey though, to feel the extremes and to face them head on. I had backed off from storms in earlier states but now was more seasoned and ready to take them on with a smile on my face.

I was exhausted and very low on water when I came across the closed down restaurant were I would have been able to fill my water bottles. The storm front had moved on and it was calm again. The shoulder was still a ragged, broken, and a sunken remnant of what it once had been. This slowed me down considerably. My mother pulled into the abandoned parking lot just a little after I had arrived. She must have sensed I would appreciate some water and had circled back for me. She had ice water and ice cream. I jumped in her camper van and enjoyed the cool refreshments. I was burnt out but resisted her call for me to pack it up for the night and head down the road with her to the gas station where we were toying with the notion of staying. The European rider in Rawlins had warned me that there was a hefty price for staying in their dirt parking lot and I was not looking forward to that. I rested with mom and thanked her for the treat. I declined her offer to drive me up the road even though she insisted it was all uphill from there. So I set out to go up and over another continental divide before exiting out into Muddy Gap.

I am glad that I rode on as it was a peaceful climb followed by some really epic terrain. The sun was starting to set and there were shadows on the road as I moved in between some mountains. There were fences erected on top of some of the higher rocks to block the wind and the traffic was almost nonexistent. The sun shown on me just a little more as I moved through the gap and out the other side. I could see up a couple draws on either side of the road and flags flapping in the breeze at the gas station ahead. Everyone was waiting for me there but they had decided not to camp at the service station. I felt the same way and thought this was as good a day as any to complete my first century ride on the journey.

I had completed my very first century ride while riding across Iowa two years before the TransAmerican Trail. It had been a very hot and somewhat windy day too. I can still remember that feeling of accomplishment it had given me and was happy to find that in myself once more. I filled up my water bottle for the last time that day and took to the road heading toward Yellowstone. It was uphill into the waning light of the last gasps of the day. Everything was gold in the brilliance of the sun and the last bright rays warmed my face as I rode on and on into the rocky wilderness. I lost track of all time and milage as I moved through the terrain alone.

I only celebrated a little as my bike computer acknowledged my hundredth mile for the day as it was not the last mile. I still had 14 more to go before the fun stopped in Jeffery City. I limped along at a slow pace even when the wind had died down. I saw the buildings of the town a good deal before I ever met up with them. They slowly grew larger and taller as the next hour dragged on. I felt ecstatic inside to have arrived once I saw the SUV in a sand parking lot next to the motel and I rode into the dirt at a fast coast. The dirt was too soft and deep for my small tires though. I spilled the bike right in front of the vehicle and went down hard. I had been in my fist wreck since leaving the East Coast. I was fine and the bike looked fine too as I picked us both up off the ground. Brianne came running out to see if I was all right and I told her not to worry. I was too tired to care really either way. I was just glad to be with my family again.

Brianne had told me that my mother had not wanted to stay there for the evening since it was barren, without power, and the mosquitos were thick. She had driven further down the road to Sweetwater Station, the next town over. Brianne left it up to me if we would meet her there for the night or if we would catch up at some point later the next day. I really wanted my mother to be included in every part of this great adventure as she had just retired and this was just as epic for her as it was for us. So we traveled into the setting sun.

My mother had unfortunately missed the small blip that was Sweetwater Station. We had no way of contacting her as there was no cell phone service out there. Conor was very concerned about grandma and he teared up as he asked us if she would make it back to camp that evening. We assured him she would be just fine and he calmed down a little. We just had to pray she was safe and comfortable where ever she had landed. She was as it turned out. She had found a very nice RV park further down the road. So much further that it took me half a day to cover those miles on my bicycle the next day. Brianne found the gentlemen who ran the camp ground at Sweetwater Station and secured a free place for us to set up for the night. He was very generous and encouraged us to participate in the festivities. Brianne and the boys did but I was really spent and so I ate my dinner with everyone and relaxed. We had parked next to a pop up camper in a field where they fogged with DEET as we set up shop. No mosquitos and the dead silence led to a very quick descent into the dream world.

I slept in until the sun woke me. Gabriel wanted to go out for his morning rounds and I noticed my mother had found us and was parked in front of our SUV. I walked Gabriel and then headed over to my mother's to inquire about her evening the night before. She was doing well and let me know that she had stayed in a really great place. We had Cheerios and coffee with her as Brianne and the boys began to stir. I helped Brianne move Conor over to Grandma's camper and then packed up for the day.

The ride out of the place was soft gravel and I took it easy after yesterday's spill. I then crossed the highway to the rest area and filled my water bottles there. They had installed a fancy bottle filling station and I quickly filled all of my bottles and then cleaned up in the bathroom sink. I brushed my teeth and washed my face with soap and water. I applied a liberal amount of beard oil to my head and beard and then combed it out. I felt fresh and the light aroma of cinnamon and patchouli from my homemade oil filled my nostrils. Just outside the bathroom there was a pleasant couple from Germany filling their water bottles. They were headed eastbound from the rest area and we swapped stories of the road.

Once back outside I saddled up and set off. I was soon treated to some awesome views and downhill grades. It took a long time to cover the 40 miles to where I was meeting everyone for lunch but it was so beautiful and there were few if any cars. The road wrapped around one red rocked formation on my left and dropped off steeply to the right where the sun rose over the flats below. I cruised faster and faster down the grade with the wind in my face and not a care in the world. I did pass the RV site where my mother had stayed but it was right before the town where we were meeting for lunch.

We ate at a Pizza Hut, which was a rare treat. My mother went to a clinic to see what they could do for some sinus pressure she was having and we all met back up at the public library. The library was large and I read two books on trains to Conor as he sat in my lap by the window. My mother must have given the man smoking outside next to the door a dirty look because he told her, "Ah don't give me that sour puss." Brianne worked on the website and my mother worked with Aaron on his speech once she had settled in. The rest rejuvenated me and I was on full power as I left for Fort Washakie.

The ride through downtown was fun as it was busier than most I had come across. There was a touristy atmosphere to it and I stopped in at the Napa auto parts store to look for lug nuts for Isosceles. I had been testing the torque on the lug nuts every 1,000 miles and had found a slightly cracked one on such a test the week before. The gentleman behind the counter said he could not help me though without one to match. I thought it would be difficult to accomplish this as Brianne and the camper were always separated from me during those parts of the day. I left empty handed and it was not far to the edge of town from there. It started to rain on me as I made it out and so I stopped to put the rain cover on my handlebar bag just before I entered the Wind River Native American Reservation. I wish it had rained longer than the 10 minutes it did because the climate had been so arid for the past few days. I was complaining about being drenched for so many days in the beginning and now I was too dry, such is life. The reservation was beautiful to ride through. I picked up some scrap metal wire in my rear derailleur but stopped before it could damage anything. A plastic yard sign got caught in my last derailleur and it had entangled itself in the spokes from there which pulled the derailleur into them causing a complete meltdown. I had to walk my bicycle the half of a mile back to work. It had taken a new derailleur and a handful of spokes to fix things. I was not too happy.

I rode past a trading post and then into the town of Fort Washakie where the grave of Sacajawea is located. I pushed on past Fort Washakie and then started to ascend another long hill into the open terrain. There was a small tailwind now and a dark cloud that just hung over me providing shade without the usual storm. I glided up and down the hills which then turned into a killer steep grade going down for a great long stretch. I felt safe at speeds above 40 miles per hour and relished the free miles I racked up without a single crank of the pedals. I soon came upon a rest stop where everyone was waiting for me. It was on top of a large rock formation after a bend in the road and overlooked vast amounts of harsh but beautiful land. I rested there and had my second lunch for the day. I was nearly asleep in the camper van when Brianne told me to get a move on as the sun was starting to get lower in the sky and we had no place to stay for the night. The rest stop forbade camping and my maps did not offer any nearby alternatives.

The next ten miles were easy enough and I thought about putting in another century ride. I stopped at a gas station in Crowheart when I saw my family parked there and to my surprise the owners told us to set up camp at the volunteer fire department across the highway. It was a great place to stay as there were mountain views in every direction. Storm cells played out far off into the distance as we ate our dinner and played Yahtzee. At some point we grew tired and all headed off to bed. My mother remarked, "There are no bugs out here." We all agreed that it had been really pleasant not to be on the menu for the mosquitos while we ate our dinner outside for once in a long while. I was growing excited now that there were only two more days of riding ahead of me before Yellowstone and the Tetons! I slept well again dreaming of what was to come.

The last day of June provided an exciting ride. The ride out from Crowheart was a gradual climb into Dubois. I left the reservation now and eventually made it into town. There was a small coffee shop right before the route turned left down the main street and I stopped in to enjoy a mocha with a cinnamon roll. The woman who owned the shop had recently opened for business within the last month and was still getting used to the flow. Some of her morning customers were irritated with the speed in which she was able to whip up hot frothed milk over dark pressed espresso and I wondered why there had to be such a hurry to everything. One would hope that a trip to get a cup of coffee in such a locale as this would be a slow relaxing part of ones morning ritual. I was content with the pace of things that morning and shared a smile and a knowing look with the others around me who were too.

I called Brianne from a small wooden table by the window and let her know where I was. There was a Napa store down the street according to Google Maps and I let her know that I would try to find the correct lug nut now that I knew what the size of the outside of it was. I took a turn through a construction site to cut through to the shop but found that the way was blocked. A worker found me and told me that I needed to head back out onto the main street and come back around as the area was torn up passed that point. I arrived at the parts store only to find out that I needed to know the inside size of the thread for the lug nut as well and left Napa empty handed again. We would just have to have the camper on hand the next time we tried. I pedaled down through town and out the other end as Brianne caught up with me. We all ate lunch together before I headed out to climb Togwotee Pass.

The road from there began to steadily climb and the sky began to grow darker as a storm system blotted out the sun. I ran into a young man named Tom from Tasmania after that and then an Aaron from Omaha, Nebraska who was riding with Tom. It was fun to talk to someone from our home town riding the TransAm. He and I had both been tracking our daily miles on the National Commuter Bicycle Challenge. I was amazed to have run into him out there. We wished each other well and started to pedal off as the black clouds began to form ominously around the mountains.

The storm started as a down pour and I became drenched over a short period of time. The road started to leach out white foam and I rode on through the frothy puddles. The terrain looked less rocky there with a fine covering of pine trees. Booming thunder started off in the distance echoing loudly across the mountains. The lightning was hidden from me, masked behind those giant mountains surrounding me. I knew the storm was going to cross paths with me soon and I pushed on. I passed by the last gas station before the serious climbing up the pass began and the storm started to get more intense. There was a sign on the side of the road flashing a warning of bears up ahead. "Stay in your vehicles," it had said and I thought that was not very helpful for a cyclist like me. The air became thinner and colder as I ascended. My arms prickled with goose bumps and I kept moving now to stay warm. The temperature dropped to 46 degrees and I could see the lightning strikes now as the storm poured over the last mountainous buttress between us. The booms and ear shattering claps came quicker and quicker as I climbed. I must have looked crazy riding up that pass. A man stopped his truck on the shoulder of the road to capture video of me as I climbed. I became a little dizzy then as I churned on the pedals in the cold wet air. I was within a mile of the summit now and my heart was in full overdrive keeping my muscles oxygenated and my core warm. I rested just for a fleeting moment as I did not want to lose the heat my body had generated from the constant pedaling. I focused on the forward movement and eventually summited the pass. It felt great to overcome this mammoth obstacle in my path and the storm subsided as I stopped to take in what I had just accomplished.

The mosquitoes set in on me almost the instant I had stopped. I whipped out some Deep Woods Off and took care of them. A couple from Switzerland were exiting an outhouse up the hill and I waited for them to come down to the road. We spoke for a moment at the pass. They had ridden here all the way from Switzerland, minus the flight across the ocean. They were on their third year of living on the road with their bicycles. The man was quiet but his companion talked with me about their current leg of the adventure. They were going to continue heading north and then cross into Canada from there. What a glorious way to live a portion of one's life out in the wild on an adventure without end. The man said he would pray for sunshine so that I could dry off and warm up. I always see them traveling forever north when I think of them.

The descent was spectacular. It was an experience that I shall never forget. I rode down out of the pass for mile after mile at 46 miles per hour. The sun did come out and warmed me as I rode faster and faster. The grade became even steeper and the pines began to blur a little as I zoomed past. A lodge and gas station appeared out of nowhere in an opening in the trees and I gripped hard on the brakes to make the turn into the parking lot. The lodge stood tall, set back off the lot and looked very cozy. I coasted over to the gas station and parked my bike along the right wall. A woman at the gas pump smiled at me as I walked around the corner to the entrance. I must have been a sight with my full beard and weathered bicycle clothing. I smiled back and walked through the door and then perused the isles for snacks. There was hot coffee, chips, and spicy canned bean dip. I talked with the clerk about how beautiful the area was as I paid and then sat down outside the door to eat and warm up with the coffee. I felt euphoric with happiness. I had summited a crazy pass in chilled air through a mean thunder storm. I took it all in and smiled.

A woman came over from the lodge carrying a large amount of drinks for the gas station. I helped her inside with them and she thanked me. "Would you like to come over to the lodge and warm yourself by the fireplace?" she asked. I did but it was time to head on down the road again. I was humbled that she would invite me into the lodge when some were even afraid to touch my hand while exchanging money after I had been riding all day in the elements. She was kind just as the gas station clerk in Virginia had been not caring that I was soaking wet and tracking water into his shop. There were many kind people in the rural places I had found.

I left the gas station parking lot glowing from the day and then quickly got up to speed as the road sharply slanted down from there. The trees began to open up and the ground shown more vegetation than the parts I had come from. I zoomed past the couple from Switzerland who must have passed me while I was shopping for snacks. Then the world opened up to me as I shot out of the mountain tops and leaned out into a very steep descent where I could see all the way down to the valley below. It was a moment of such epic sensory overload that it felt like a dream. Toward the bottom I crossed paths with some travelers heading up the pass the other direction. They waved at me as I flew past and I put out my left hand in a controlled wave so as not to end up flying in a bad way. Up ahead of me the Grand

Daniel McDonald

Tetons rose out of the earth like jagged teeth. The air became warmer as I rode down further and further. Camp was waiting for me just as the terrain flattened out and I had to start pedaling again. Brianne, the boys, and my mother were in Jackson Hole enjoying the sites but I had a spare set of keys for the camper in my handlebar bag. I hung up my things to dry outside and deployed our solar cells to charge Isosceles' batteries. Then I fell asleep totally spent from such an epic day.

We had dinner when everyone returned and the night started to become cold. The mosquitoes were thick and ruthless so we stayed inside when possible. I cuddled the boys as we all drifted off to sleep.

Our phone batteries died during the night as we slept. I slept in having no alarm, which was good because it was cold out. Too cold to start without a little sun to warm my face for sure. I snuggled Aaron and Conor close drifting in and out of sleep for a while longer. The sun and Gabriel eventually got me out of bed and I took him for a walk around the camp ground. The morning was still crisp but not as bad in the sun's warmth. The mosquitoes from last night must have been sleeping off a blood hangover because they were nowhere in sight. I had some hot coffee and cereal with my mother and then started to get on the move.

The ride into Teton National Park was beautiful. The Tetons were jagged, snowy, and magical in the morning light. I rode up to the ranger booth and found that bicycles cost $20 to get into the park. At least the money goes to something cool. I rode into the park and found the views of the Tetons just kept getting better the closer I got to them. I eventually passed a majestic lake where the mountains appeared to rise out of the clear blue water. Later down the rode I enjoyed some more coffee with a cheese Danish outside of a park store. I sat in the sun out on the picnic bench and just enjoyed being there. I had really been looking forward to experiencing the Tetons and Yellowstone for years. I was there and riding my bicycle through them to boot! I came across a choke point where I waited in line behind RV's, cars, and all manners of transportation as we passed into Yellowstone. The ranger at the booth asked, "Have you ever ridden through Yellowstone before?" I had not and told him so. "Those dents in the railings up ahead didn't put themselves there." He probably thought it was a silly risk to take, to make the ride through this heavily trafficked park. I thanked him for the warning and pedaled on. The road began to narrow and I was in the traffic riding the white line. The traffic did not let up either and we all shared the road. It wound back and forth like a snake through the trees and soon I saw the large dents in the guard rails that kept arrant vehicles from going over the edge into the rapids far down below. Brianne, the boys, and my mother had explored the park ahead of me and found another great place to spend the night near a lake deep in the trees. I began to get some pretty bad acid reflux as I climbed another continental divide and my throat burned. I stopped to rest at the top and sipped water to soothe my esophagus. There were other riders out and I crossed paths with them coming and going. Some rode in the center of the lane and others along the line such as I did. I can see both sides of the debate on this one as taking the lane makes you more visible and something that a vehicle needs to pass instead of riding dangerously close to without moving over. I feared the texting drivers and tried to stay as far over as safely possible.

The sky darkened and poured out cold rain on me for the second day in a row. The vehicles that were passing me had now come to a stop as the traffic began to back up. I passed them on the right and made my way down the road. The camp site was another four miles ahead and my riding was done for the day at just about 49 miles. I loved rolling rest days as we had come to call days less than 65 miles. I could cover 90 miles before 1PM at this point if I started early enough. Brianne and I cooked dinner as my mother entertained the boys. A camp host knocked on our door to see if we belonged in the spot we were parked in. She was attempting to give it away to another group thinking we were intruding upon an abandoned but paid for spot. We let her know that we were the ones that had paid for it earlier and she went on her way. I found it a bit comical that they resell spots like that but I guess there are so many visitors each night that they need to ensure every spot is used regardless of how many times it was paid for. We headed over a loop to where my mother and the boys were to enjoy our pasta. After a relaxing meal we took a hike to Lewis Lake. It was so clean and wide open. You could see the bottom of the lake for a good length as you looked out and down upon it. I took off my shoes and walked into the water. It was cold and felt great. The boys threw rocks into the water and we began to attract very large mosquitoes. My mother sprayed the air around them with DEET but they must have had that spice before in their meals as they seemed unaffected. After our hike we went back to the camper to bed down for the evening. Our neighbors brought back some foraged wood and started a campfire. They were on their honey moon and were camping without a tent next to the fire. I looked over my maps for the next day's ride and they advised that I should ride only in the early hours of the morning

I Like to Ride

around Yellowstone to avoid the heavy traffic. I planned on getting up with the sun. I was going to be in West Yellowstone by the end of the next day and this would put me just across the border into Montana.

Montana

I arose a lot earlier than normal. The morning air was crisp and Gabriel wanted to walk about as usual. Our neighbors had a good fire going and were tending to it. It smelled great. They had put up a rain flap and had slept under it near the fire. I admired that kind of camping. I prepped the camper for an easy departure and then packed up my bike with the days gear. I coasted off down the loop to the entrance of the camp site. The host was out walking her dog and she flagged me down to talk. "Where were you hiding last night?" she inquired? I laughed and reminded her that she had knocked on our door. She smiled and wished me a happy day of riding. I would wager to guess that she finds a good number of cyclists camped up in the woods on any given summer's night. Who could blame them though in such a beautiful place. There is something to be said for camping off the trail deep in between the pines. My mother was down the hill and I stopped in to see her before heading out. It was great to get the chance to connect with her so much. At this point I had delayed my early departure enough, so I hugged her and set out once more.

I rode out onto the main road that goes through Yellowstone. The route offers much climbing but with very cool features to occupy the climber. The trees have a half alive feel to them as you get closer to the geysers and super hot springs. There are many different points of interest, even just off the main road. I detoured into Grant Village to see what was over there. I thought that I might catch a meal or get some coffee. I ended up meeting an adventurous couple from Germany at a service station. We spoke of things to come for each other and our love of hot springs. They looked like they were really enjoying themselves. We took pictures together and then I set off back in the direction that I had come from. Next I was headed towards Old Faithful. There were some good climbs on the way and the riding went by slowly. I crested one such climb and found a small pond filled with water lilies. One good thing about touring on a bicycle is that you can stop just about anywhere to get off and explore without the need to find a parking spot. I took full advantage of this and enjoyed the scenery before moving on. I cruised down the road and onto flatter terrain from there. At one point I passed a pedestrian walkway and regretted not taking it. I had a hunch that it led to somewhere I wanted to be and was right. I crossed paths with it again while following the signs for Old Faithful. The area around old faithful was very touristy. My mother told me later that it was much different when she had visited as a young girl. Once you get on the boardwalk you are treated to several geysers. Old Faithful goes off every 90 minutes or so but I was lucky enough to see one called Beehive go off as I waited there for my family to catch up with me. It was worth stopping to see for sure. One of the rangers asked me to move my bicycle back out into the parking lot after I was done watching Old Faithful as they did not allow them on the boardwalk. I had missed the sign and let him know I would do just that after the show. Ten minutes later another ranger approached me with the same news but wanted me to move it right away. I let her know what the previous ranger had said and the folks around me collaborated with my story but she was having none of it and off I went. I was so worried that I would miss the geyser and yet was torn about my bicycle disappearing too. I propped it up against a tree in eye shot of the board walk and ran back. I was just in time to see it but had lost my choice seat in the front. At least I could keep an eye on my bicycle from where I stood. Old Faithful teased us on several occasions over the next ten minutes and then erupted with spectacular glory. The boiling hot water sprayed up high into the sky and rained down for some time before petering out.

Brianne, the boys, and my mother arrived soon after and we had lunch in the camper van out in the RV parking lot. After lunch we all watched Old Faithful go off together. Brianne and the boys loved it! I held Conor on my shoulders and lifted Aaron up in front of me. One boy held in each arm. After the show we explored the information center and I am so glad we did as I was able to see videos and pictures of many of the hot springs that I would miss as I stuck to the main route through the park. It was time to ride again and I made for West Yellowstone as the day became hot.

Along the way I saw a wondrous hot spring, a crazy landscape created by the cauldron environment, and more geysers far off in flat fields. The park rangers had to go out and get several tourists back onto safe ground as they had ventured out into the open landscape to get a closer look at some of the geysers. A man had recently met with a bad end doing the same thing. The ground around the springs and geysers is not always solid and can be just a crust covering an acidic boiling pool of unfriendliness. The rangers brought the ambulance with them just in case it turned into a recovery mission instead of a lecture. The ride to West Yellowstone from there was beautiful as it curved through streams and canyons. The wind picked up and I began to have some trouble with my bike wanting to whip left and right a little too easily. I thought it was the wind but it turned out to be an issue with the nut that held the front fork in place while allowing it a little free play. There were people wading in streams and the sun began to set creating a reflective shine across the wind spun waters. I rode on and passed a tiny wooden sign that said entering Montana. I guess I should have captured the moment on my camera because that was the only sign I found. I exited the park sad that it had gone by so fast and rolled out into the town.

I checked the RV park for everyone but they were not there. Next I headed to Dairy Queen for a large monster cookie blizzard. As I wolfed it down another cross country cyclist came up to me and struck up a conversation. He was eastbound and was riding his own route which composed of the TransAm and cities he had wanted to see. Shawn was his name and he enjoyed DQ as much as I did. He was kind enough to let me use his cell phone to call Brianne. Mine died and the cord to charge it was with Brianne. She did not answer with it being a strange California number but I figured that we would find each other eventually. After that I headed over to the intersection where I had come into town and waited. There were hundreds of people walking here and there up and down the street shopping. After waiting there for a half hour I headed to the library and found everyone on the way! There was nowhere to stay in town but a Forest Service campground down the way had a single spot open still if we hurried and were lucky enough to beat others to it. We did get the last spot and it was an awesome campground. My mother said we should have stayed for a few more days there; she was right but my mind was always telling me to keep moving forward. We had pancakes and eggs for dinner, played Yahtzee, and fell asleep.

I ended up staying at our camp site until almost 10AM. The morning was beautiful. We were completely surrounded by trees and it was good to have breakfast with everyone. The morning ride was supposed to be all downhill from there or so said my maps, it was but into the wind. The going was slow and my bicycle was acting funny still in that it turned left and right way too easily. The route turned off down a road that wrapped around a large lake. There were camping spots everywhere you looked but no services for miles. I eventually turned down a dirt side road and stopped. I got out my crescent wrench and proceeded to try to resolve my flighty front wheel problem. I was going mad trying to control the bicycle at this point and just knew that I was going to go down hard on a fast downhill if I did not address it now. I gave the fork a good tightening and then headed into the trees to take a rest break.

I packed up my wrench and got back out onto the main road again. The work I had done helped a little but not as much as I had hoped it would. I decided to try a higher air pressure in the tires the next day to see if they were low enough to cause some trouble. I found that really low air pressure causes all sorts of instability while trying to ride a little on my first flat back in Colorado.

Further down the path I rode through an area where the lake was tilted by an earthquake. It was so cool. The skeletons of long dead lodge pole pines stuck up out of the lake. The scenery was beautiful. I pedaled up through a tight little pass after the lake, then out the other side into a foothill environment. You could see for miles on end up to the next large mass of earth that rose high up into the horizon. The road started to head down along a stream. I found some rest at a stop near the stream where fly fishers were casting the day away. I sat out on a bench in the front eating chips while people came and went. Storm clouds began to roll in as I laid there looking up at the sky. After quite some time I decided it was time to head out. I got myself up and on the saddle again. Brianne and the boys pulled in just as I was leaving and she made me a peanut butter and jelly sandwich for the road. With kisses for all I was off to beat the storm, which was threatening to make my afternoon rough from the looks of it. Silly me, bikes do not tend to go fast enough to outrun mother nature.

Two fronts collided at the exact place where I was riding. They created a massive tailwind that propelled me at 27 miles per hour down the road for a good 10 miles before I was hit by just as massive of a cross wind. The rain stung as it pelted my face and the wind threatened to knock me off the road with every gust but I rode on. Eventually the storm calmed and riding returned to normal. I passed by a group of Southbound cyclists taking shelter and waved at them. On I went until I reached Ennis which was to be our stopping point for the evening. There was no viable place there for us though and we ate a meal together in the Lions Park. The Lions organization had built many parks along the route in the most rural of places. I always found them to be of great value. After a long rest in the park we headed to the vehicles to get a move on further down the route. My mother found a large red ticket on her windshield and we read it to see what the damages were going to be. It was just a move it now or else kind of ticket, so we moved it. The good news about adding milage onto the day was that we would be further towards our goal but I had to bike up another pass to get there.

I met two cyclists heading to RAGBRAI and they gave me homemade chocolate chip cookies. What a great couple of guys! They decided it would be more fun to ride their bicycles to the starting point and then complete the tour before returning home the way they had come. They had recognized my RAGBRAI jersey and flagged me down. We chatted for about 30 minutes and then said our goodbyes. I bet they had a great time in Iowa. I know I did when I rode through there two years before. I stopped at a gas station to pick up some candy and ice cream before leaving town. I had started to use candy back in Missouri to boost my sugar levels while climbing passes. I always made sure to have a bag of cinnamon bears or something like them before doing any mountain climbing. Maybe it was the sweet reward that kept me pedaling but I like to think it was the energy boost they gave me. Ennis was fun and now it was time to take the pass.

The road out of town started to rise right after the gas station. The grade started to become challenging as I passed the museum on the outside of town and then became brutal over time. This pass had no relief until I had weaved in and out of the mountainous hills for a good long hour, finally reaching the upper parts. I had to stop and rest when I reached the point where it snaked to the left. I was thoroughly exhausted doing this kind of pass work so late in the day. I knew that I had to keep going though and that every stroke of the pedal got me closer to the summit. I reached an overlook and stopped to look out on where I had come from. Everything below looked tiny and far away. The sun was starting to hang lower on the horizon and I needed to keep moving or I would be riding in the dark at some point. I had the lights for it but would rather be safe in camp when the sun had finally set. As I was turning around to leave my mother pulled up in the camper van and we greeted each other. She told me that I was still a ways off from the summit and offered a ride. I declined but stayed a little longer to talk with her and rest. She told me she would pick up some dinner for us all in the next town over and meet me at the camp they had found a few more towns after that. I still had a ways to go before I was done.

Further up the pass I came upon a cross that had been placed on the cliff's edge. It had a Christmas wreath around it and the name of the person who had gone off the road. There had been many crosses along the route but this one saddened me more than most as it had occurred during the holidays. I reached one false summit and then continued to the top after a 2,200 foot climb in elevation from the bottom. The down hill was just as steep but did not last as long as the up part had. A car came into my lane as they passed another and I had to take the shoulder to avoid being creamed. It was a good thing I had my wits about me. No cross for me on the side of the road that day. I raced down through Virginia City and out the other side. I had a good head of steam that lasted all the way until I reached camp just before Alder. Ninety-Two miles of riding some awesome terrain. My mother did not find anything vegetarian for dinner in Virginia City and so we cooked in camp. Dinner was ice cold beer, carrots, fruit, rice, and beans. We all ate our fill and enjoyed the beautiful scenery as rain fell from clouds far off in the distance. The dusk sky was lit up pink and red as the sun began to hide under the horizon. Tomorrow was going to be a short day or as I liked to call them, a rolling rest day.

It was the Fourth of July and I awoke well rested in our campsite. It had been a quiet night and I had a shower in the bath house before enjoying breakfast. The road from there was empty and I cruised on into a small town with a gas station in the center of its main street. I stopped in and bought some doughnuts to enjoy along with a soda. I ate them outside next to the pumps and looked out over the town. There were shuttered businesses almost everywhere you looked. One of them had been gone for a long time, as the window chalk spoke of having a great 2015.

I left that small town riding out alone down its main street and turned out onto the open road again. There was a rest stop with a cyclist lodge not to far down the road and it was really neat. They had built a bunk house there next to the stream and it would have made for a must stop overnight had I been out on this adventure alone. I filled my water bottles and moved on. I was heading out into farm, ranch, and homestead lands now. I did cross paths with a small log cabin coffee shop in the middle of nowhere but was still full from my stop in the prior town. I pedaled on into the countryside and the wind began to pick up.

The tall grass in the fields to my right looked like water as it moved in the wind. I stopped to watch, captivated by the peace it brought me. The wind did make for hard travel though and the air was extremely dry now. I was sufficiently tired as I crossed an abandoned truck weigh station just a mile outside of Dillon. They were all abandoned along this route from the East to here from what I had seen.

The town of Dillon was hot and a bit dusty with the wind blowing as it was. I stopped in at McDonalds to take down a large vanilla shake and French fry. I updated my blog and uploaded pictures using the wifi. I called Brianne to arrange a meeting point in the Safeway parking lot next door. After my salty calorie laden meal I coasted over to the RV parking spots in the rear of the lot and waited under a shade tree. Another cyclist rode up to me with a good sized card board box resting on his handlebars. We started up a conversation and I found out that he was a teacher who had been spending his summers off exploring the country by bicycle. This was not his first long tour and he was shipping some items that he was not going to need at this point in his journey back home to save on weight. He was staying at a KOA in town and wanted me to swing by later. I let him know I had no idea where we were staying for the night but I would certainly try to do so if I could. Unfortunately, we stayed further down the road on the very edge of town and I never saw him again. He looked like he could have used the company and I felt bad about not being able to share an evening around a campfire learning about his life. I do enjoy being able to see life through the lens of other's experiences. I hope he enjoyed the rest of his journey.

The RV park we picked to stay in was perfect. We had no power or water as those spots were all taken but the owner had us park in the tent area under a shade tree and I believe those spots were much better than the gravel lot type RV spots. We all enjoyed dinner together, showered, and walked around the area. It was a wonderful evening and one of the better fourth of Julys I can remember.

The next day started out early as the sun began to rise. The temperature was in the 30s. I was cold and stiff. My blue jacket kept my core nice and warm and the climbing that started right away turned up the heat as I burned through some calories. The sun was beginning to shine on my face now. How I love that feeling on cold early morning rides. I rode up a very long stretch at a slight grade as the homes began to thin out along the road. The sun had risen enough now to offer more warmth, causing me to perspire. There is a fine balance of body warmth to perspiration one must maintain in such climates. If you are too warm and soak your shirt with perspiration you can become even colder when you stop moving. It is best to stay warm but just slightly. I removed my jacket and felt the crisp air on my damp skin beneath my Jersey. The dry air eventually made me feel more comfortable and the temperature crept into the 60s for most of the day. The first pass was a bit of a climb and it took me past Bannack State Park. The road leading into the park was dirt and I skipped it. I wish I had explored it though as another westbound rider that I met later near Missoula told me how he went down that road and into a ghost town. He really enjoyed the experience and I recommend you do the same should you find yourself on this journey too. Once I summited the pass I zoomed down hill at great speeds. I had to wrap up in my jacket again as the wind from my forward momentum chilled my body. The pedal free coasting soon ended though and it was back to climbing the next pass.

I met my family on the side of the road just as the second pass began to get steeper. My mother made an egg salad sandwich for me and we all enjoyed the early morning sun together. There was a ranch down a draw below us and I watched as a rancher worked on the property. A sheriff rode by and paused before moving on down the road. I imagine we looked a little out of place. They may also have been making sure we did not need any assistance before moving on with their day. We wrapped things up and I was off to conquer another pass.

The climb up the second pass was tougher. It wound around the mountain side and kept on increasing in grade and intensity. A road crew worker zipped past me in a four wheel cart as they sprayed the weeds on the side of the road. There were signs all over warning of invasive weeds. There were even weed inspection sites for hay on trailers as well. I was soon treated to a spectacular view as I crested the summit. My favorite parts of the trip were summiting passes as they gave you a real feeling of raw accomplishment along with breathtaking views for your reward. From the top it was a long descent at great speed. The wind whipped in my face as I grasped the handlebars and settled in for the long ride. The road curved left and then straightened out again before curving right alongside another mountain. I was down in another wide valley before too long and the pedaling resumed.

The two towns I went through after that did not offer me much of a reason to linger as they were very small and had few services. I rode through some broken glass between the two of them and cursed the moron who thought it belonged there on the road. About five miles later I was changing the inner tube on the front tire. I thought I had been lucky but sadly that was not the case. The mosquitoes let me know they were there in number as I worked on getting back on the road. I did visit a small grocery store in Wisdom to eat Fritos with bean dip washing them down with a Coke. A dust devil whipped up in front of the store and let me know that I was in for a windy finish to the day. There were only 16 more miles to go but it was into a strong headwind and up some more hills.

I chugged along at eight to ten miles per hour for a very long time. The road began to head into some more mountains. I came across two riders heading eastbound and waved at them as they zipped past down the last of their descent. I typically did not stop to talk to others on a descent either. I climbed out of the rocky parts of the valley and into the pines again. The trees were very tall and the wind lost some steam in them. I was really worn out now and just wanted to be in camp. It was so peaceful though in the forest and the wind sounded soothing now that it was no longer hindering my progress. I was riding next to a creek and the sound of the water over the rocks added to the lulling feeling of the place. About six miles into the forest was our campsite. It was nestled into the tall trees across the creek and we shared it with very few other souls. After dinner we took a hike through the forest by a stream. The water was so clear you could see every stone under its babbling current. What a wonderful ending to a day of climbing passes and fighting the wind. The next day we would make for Missoula, home of Adventure Cycling and my cousins. It would be over a century ride away too.

The morning air was cold as I awoke in the forest and stepped outside Isosceles. My bike said 35 degrees when I plugged the computer in its place on the handlebars and I could see my breath as I exhaled. It was hard to tell how accurate that little computer was but it was cold. I wore two pairs of gloves and my jacket. I worked on a spoke that had loosened up and then trued the back wheel before lubing the chain. I had been lubing the chain almost every day since leaving the East Coast as I liked to keep it running smoothly across the gears. I filled the tires to 70 psi and packed up my riding gear for the day. There was about 108 miles between me and Missoula and I was ready to get cracking at it. I woofed down yogurt with blueberries and then a cup of coffee with my mother before hitting the trail. She was usually awake and ready to have breakfast with me before I headed out for the day.

There was one pass ahead of me and then an entire day of down hill into the valley. There were dear and birds out in the crisp morning air. I saw bear scat but no bear which made me glad. I had been told they could run faster than I could pedal on a flat road with the wind at my back and this did not make me feel comfortable. I was riding uphill now and would have no chance to escape. I could raise my bike above my head to make myself look bigger. Thank God I never had to cross that bridge. The ride up into the pass was beautiful as the lodge pole pines surrounded me and my mind recalled Christmas with the cold smell of pine in the air. It began to drizzle cold rain and I was glad for the jacket and gloves that kept me warm and somewhat dry. The pass was not so bad and it ended with a steep descent. My head began to ache in the frigid air as I climbed to speeds of 45 miles per hour. I had to stop at the Idaho border and tie my bandana around my head to protect it from the wind. I took the opportunity to snap a photo of me at the Montana welcome sign since I had missed the one in West Yellowstone. I stepped into the woods to take care of business and only then noticed the rest area sign after coming back out. It was right across the road and I went over there to freshen up for the day. There was a gentleman cleaning it who warned me not to get the bleach solution he was mopping the floor with on my shoes as it was caustic. He then proceeded to slosh it all around and it ended up on my shoes anyway. I chuckled a bit as I left.

I Like to Ride

The ride down the mountain was awesome except for the loose gravel along the shoulder. It curved down and around the large rock formations towering over me as I descended and then straightened out for a moment. I stopped in at a cabin rental and service stop to get some candy. The woman behind the counter told me to eat breakfast first and then I could have some candy. I turned toward the back of the shop and there was a young woman cooking up short order eggs and hash browns. I had some with a cup of coffee. The eggs were great but the hash browns and biscuits were rewarmed from who knows when. I was happy to eat it though. The gentleman from the rest stop stopped in and had breakfast across from me. I smiled up at him as he came in and he went about his business. I used the wifi to read the weather report and then the news. I had not cared to know what was going on in the world around me for some time now but it was fun to check in just this once. I polished off the rest of my meal and drank another heavily creamed coffee before tipping the cook at the counter and then heading back into the candy isle. I stocked up on candy for the long day. The woman behind the register complained about her cough and sore throat as I paid. I was not too thrilled about the prospect of catching her cold but I was also sure my immune system was up to the task. I had found that living outside and exercising daily kept me from getting sick while I was in Iraq and it held true here too. I left the cabin rental place and ventured forth around the next bend.

The ride down the steepest grades took me through towering mountains studded with lodge pole pines. The rocks poked out at the road and I weaved around them. About ten miles later I rolled out onto a flatter down hill by cabins and a stream.

The air warmed a little into the 50s and I kept the jacket on but packed up the gloves. The air continued to warm up gradually throughout the rest of the day but never got over 70. I stopped in Darby for an egg salad sandwich at a gas station/Laundromat/casino. I ate outside on a bench using my bike rack as a table. The wind picked up and the temperature dropped a bit. The flags at the park across the street told me that a moderate headwind awaited my departure. I called my father to see how he had been holding up back in Omaha. I let him know not to worry about not being able to get ahold of mom as there was no service back where they still were. When I rode on it was into a heavy head wind.

The rode slanted slightly down hill most of the day but the wind made it feel quite the opposite. Brianne and my mother passed me about 50 miles in and I met up with them further down the road at a gas station. I added some oil to the SUV, which had a small leak and needed a watchful eye. We ate peanut butter and jelly sandwiches before I was off again into the wind. I passed by another wild fire where helicopters came and went with bags of fire retardant. I could not see the smoke through the clouds as a storm front had moved in. I battled periodic rain and more heavy winds from there on and throughout most of the rest of the day. The traffic was very heavy but I was blessed with a wide shoulder to ride on and at one point a very long bike path too. The bike path wound up and down along the road and switched from one side to the other making it a longer way to get to Missoula but a safer one for sure. I traded it in favor of the road on occasion to speed things up.

I met three cyclists eastbound from New York City at a gas station. We headed to a McDonalds in Lolo to wait out the latest downpour. One of the girls had learned how to fix her bicycle from her father who was a bike mechanic. The guy had struck out on this adventure after wanting to do it for several years. He had approached his wife about it and she was not on board in the least bit. Later on when they separated he took it as a sign that he should go. We talked about people we had met along the way and I was glad to hear that they all had spent an evening with Micheal, who we had met that first night in at the church in Virginia. He had been doing well and had moved too fast for them to keep up with. Brianne would call him later for me to see how things were going and he told her that he was riding all day and resting at night to cover as much ground as possible so that he could get home to his family. He finished well before I did and probably could have placed somewhere in the middle of the pack if he had participated in the race.

After leaving the McDonalds the wind jumped back and forth from tail to head. It rained for a stint and then let up for a while. I tried to stay in the tailwind part of the pattern for the remainder of the day. The road into Missoula was heavy with traffic and it got progressively worse as I entered the city. One truck rolled coal on me, pouring out a dark cloud of diesel exhaust. The rest of the cars rode just a foot away from me. There were no shoulders in the city and the storm drains caused me to need to ride out into the lane. Brianne was at the Chevy dealership getting the fan fixed on the radiator and my mother was with my cousins Laura and Tim. I rode across town and had to use Google Maps to reach the Adventure Cycling office. I was sad to find it closed for the day. I would not be returning and so missed my opportunity to meet the staff there and have my picture taken. I called my mother for a pick up and my cousin Tim came out to get me. I had not seen him since Brianne and my wedding which was eight years ago. He was in good spirits and we talked as we headed back to his home up in the foothills around the city. We all met back up at their place and had a great meal. Tim had me sample some local beers which were great. The pizza was NewYork style and tasted brick oven fired. We stayed up late talking about everything and had a very relaxing evening. Seeing family in Missoula was a much better treat then getting to see the Adventure Cycling office. We let the evening get really late and then had to say goodbye. Tim noticed that my seat post had cracked and was wobbly as he helped me out to the camper van. He was an avid mountain biker and had plenty of seat posts in the garage. He wanted to give me one of his but the tube was too thick for my frame. I thanked him for the kind gesture. Tim and Laura gave me a gift basket of energy bars, gel blocks, wool riding socks, gloves, and water bottles. They were great to us and I will always remember our visit fondly.

We spent the night at an RV park off the interstate. The boys loved the theme of it but Brianne and I felt it was not worth the price or very kid friendly for that matter. The next day was a rest day as we ran around town to prep for the journey ahead. The boys got to play at a castle themed local park and I stopped in at REI to purchase a new seat post. Once we were all ready we headed back to the route outside of the city around Lolo. We traveled on a short distance to a campground on route and set up in a double long spot where both RVs could fit, one behind the other. The site was backed up to a hill in the forest and gave us a little nook to spend the night. The next day I would ride over another pass and into Idaho.

I Like to Ride

Idaho

In the morning I rode down the hill from our campsite on my new seat post. It took me a little while on it to get the feel for it as I had been riding thousands of miles on the one that had cracked. I could not remember the moment it had started to fail but it did have a good wobble to it by the time Tim looked at it and found it was no longer fit for service. The sun was out and I had a smile on my face as I moved down the heavily forested road toward Lolo Hot Springs. Every now and then a large truck would pass me and give me pause for concern but no close calls.

When I reached Lolo Hot Springs I came upon the remnants of what must have been the most epic pirate party to have taken place in these parts. There was a man passed out in a folding chair at the entrance and not a soul was stirring this early. There were props and tents all around giving it a tropical vibe. I attended such parties back in Omaha on the River City Star, an old school paddle boat, and at bars with friends of ours while Brianne and I had dated. None of them held a candle to what must have taken place there as we slept in our camp miles down the road. It was kind of strange that we did not hear them even from as far away as we were but we slept great and I bet they did too.

After the hot springs came the pass. I was getting really good at passes by now and I do not remember it being particularly hard. I stopped in at the rest stop at the summit and really enjoyed the single occupancy log cabin feel to it. Each restroom had heaters, which was awesome as it was a bit chilly at the top of the pass. I bundled up for the descent and then took off. I waved at a few motorcycles that passed me; they usually waved back too. They headed on down the hill and I followed at my top speed.

I eventually reached a sign that warned of no services for many miles ahead. The Lochasa Lodge was my last shot at filling my water bottles and getting a bite to eat until supper and there was no way I was going to miss it. I am so glad that I stopped in. The lodge would have really put Brianne off as it was full of animal skins and taxidermy. These things do not tend to bother me much though and I liked the ambiance of the lodge. I was led to a table near the fire place where the bikers from earlier were having their breakfast. They were an adventuresome looking lot and I admired them. It would be enjoyable to ride around the backroads of the country someday with just Brianne and myself after the boys were older and leading independent lives of their own. Just us, the bike, and a bivy cover. Maybe a little propane stove and a mess kit too but you get the gist of it. One of the bikers came over to talk with me as I drank my coffee. He was impressed with the way I had climbed the pass on just a bicycle and thought my journey sounded great. With that they all paid their waiter and left as they must have been there for some time before I caught up with them. I ordered blueberry pancakes, hash browns, eggs, and kept the coffee coming. The food was impressive. In fact it was the best such combo that I had since leaving Yorktown.

The rest of the day took me along the Lochsa River. It was truly a paradise composed of clear water, rapids, hiking trails, and fishing. People were outdoors everywhere along the route enjoying nature. I began to use the trailheads as landmarks to see where I was on my map. I pedaled through the pines along the river the rest of the day. I eventually came across the campground we had selected to meet up and rode in to look for my family. They were not down any of the loops. I spent a good

hour looking here and there for them finally coming to the conclusion that they had not arrived yet. This was strange as I had
not crossed paths with them at all yet that day. So I rode back to
the entrance and sat there eating chips and drinking from my
water bottles. If you wait somewhere long enough something is
bound to happen and this place was no exception.

An off white sedan rolled up slowly in front of where I was
sitting and I starred at its black tinted windows as it sat there
for a moment. Even the front was fully tinted and I could not
see inside. I sat there and munched on chips waiting to see
what came next. The rear passenger door opened up and a
woman exited the vehicle with a hiking pack. She shut the door
and the car backed out turning around before leaving the way
it had come. The woman walked up to me and asked me if I
thought it was strange that the man in the vehicle who had giv-
en her a lift up there had asked her if she had wanted to burn
off any extra calories in the car with him before she went on her
hike. I found the conversation a little disturbing. I let her know
I was waiting there for my wife and children. She told me she
was married as well and was living up in the woods on the hiking trails. I wished her well and she went on her way. A little
while later a gentleman approached me as he and his children
came up from swimming in the river. We struck up a conversation and I found out he was also an Information Technology
Director. We swapped stories for about and hour until Brianne
and my mother pulled up. I wished him and his family a great
camping trip and ran over to Brianne to tell her how glad I was
that she had found me. There was no cell phone service out
there and I was starting to think I was going to have to hit the
road again to find them up until they had arrived. We all head-

ed back to the furthest loop and set up camp at the very end. It was a wonderful place to spend the night. We walked down to the river to explore it before heading to bed.

The next day I rode out into the early morning. There was a heavy fog and you could not see the mountains that surrounded us. The pines rose up and then disappeared. It was cool out. I pedaled down the loop and out onto the road that crossed the bridge on the way back to the main one. There was no traffic and I cruised down the first descent along the river. Before long I was passing men fishing and small campsites near the river. This was a beautiful and pristine part of America that had not been overdeveloped or commercialized. I would have found its ups and downs more challenging had it been the first month of the trip but I was well prepared for it now.

I rolled onto the Nezperce Reservation as I came out of the heavy forest. The road was surrounded by large treeless mountains that appeared to crumble, aged by time. I came across a rider from England who was just in his second state of the journey to Yorktown, Virginia from Astoria. We talked about the quiet beauty of the place we were in and I let him know that there was so much for his eyes to behold across this great nation. He was enjoying the American hospitality and vast open lands that were on the route. I wished him a safe journey and he congratulated me on my near finish of such an epic undertaking. I had to chuckle as the roles had been reversed when I came across Steve as he was near his finish back in the first week. I wonder if I looked as seasoned as Steve had.

From there I wandered on to Kooskia where I stopped in at a gas station for a bean and cheese burrito along with a soda.

I Like to Ride

The woman behind the counter was pleasant and talked with me about all the racers who had stopped in to see her as they made their way into the interior of the country from Oregon. Some of them had been riding over 240 miles at a clip before resting. I let her know about the woman who had won this year and she was glad to hear it. She told me that I should take my snack over to the city park where it was green. I thanked her but the road was calling me, so I finished my lunch and moved on.

Stites was the next town over and I pedaled there quickly. There was more traffic here compared to what I had been in for a while. There were small homes along the way and then I found myself on the main street of the town. A festival was going on and there were people out in the street enjoying the fresh air. I enjoyed watching them come and go with beverages in hand as some men played horseshoes across from the market. My mind was so occupied by the festival that I missed my turn and found myself outside of town on the wrong route. I studied my map for a moment to see where I had gone wrong. I decided that I needed to cross the bridge near the market. So I turned around and pedaled back through the party making the correct course adjustment when I came across the horseshoes pit once more. The other side of the river contained a small neighborhood and an older back road that started to climb almost right away. I soon came across my next turn onto a road called Lamb Grade. More like lion grade if you ask me. There was nothing lamb about the grade of that road. I toiled along the first part of the road where it switched back here and there going up the near vertical mountainous hill side. I reached a lone cherry tree after coming around a switch back and stopped to rest there as I stared up an even more impressive grade going straight up the mountain. The tree was full of ripe cherries and I was tempted to eat them but was unsure if they belonged to anyone up the road so I left them alone. I took a long swig of water from my bottle and then started up the more grueling part of the road. I was in my most forgiving gears and still had to find the strength to crawl up that grade. The road was cracked and broken in places giving me micro goals to set my sights on as I put my head down and worked. My heart let me know that it had kicked into overdrive as it began to sound off loudly in my ears. I worked myself ill as I climbed and climbed Lamb Grade Road. I had to stop and rest as the road turned and wrapped around the mountain side. I was so winded that it took me a very long time to recover. A delivery van zoomed past me. They must have thought I was a little crazy to be out there riding up that road. I thought the same at that moment. I recomposed myself and started to work again.

The top of the road crossed paths with a warehouse of sorts that must have burned to the ground. There was a truck parked next to it that was nothing more than a melted heap of metal. It looked post apocalyptic there on the top of that massive climb. There was some beauty in it sitting up there all alone. I moved on down the road, which had become only a slight grade at this point thank God. The terrain opened up into vast fields where the sun was starting to set, casting long rays of brilliant light across the expanse. I could see a storm moving in off in the distance and knew I would be in for a ride.

The storm set in with heavy rain and I began to get a little chilled. I was soon drenched to the bone. The thunder started to match the lightning strikes. I had been taught to count the flash to boom as a child giving a rough estimate of how many miles the strikes were from my position. They counted down from 10 to right over my head at one point. It was a little terrifying to be out in the open when they struck in the fields around me. None of them came near the road and I was spared a crispy ending to my long journey. The storm moved on and I rolled up and down the hills that stood between me and the town where we had planned on spending the night.

I came into the North end of Grangeville by an old RV park that looked closed down. I made the correct turn into a neighborhood that eventually took me onto the main street where I stopped to rest under a canopy in front of a store. I called Brianne to let her know I was safe and nearby. She let me know that they had found a great RV park on route just outside of town and to ride that way. The town was small and I rode out to some construction on the end where I had to wait for traffic to die down before they would let me on the shoulder across a sharp drop in the pavement. I carried my bicycle in and out of the ditch and then hopped back on once safely on the other side. The smell of tar was sharp in the air and the sun had come back out just as it was leaving the horizon for the night.

I reached the RV park and had to hop off the bike as the road turned into heavy gravel. I knew not to ride on this type of surface for its tendency to hide ruts in the hard packed clay beneath. So I walked the bike into the park and found Isosceles and my mother's camper van. We all enjoyed dinner together as the sun set and then took showers over in the club house. The showers were beautifully tiled but slippery. Aaron lost his footing and fell backwards hitting his head as he fell. He was inconsolable for about 30 minutes afterwards but thankfully no serious injury had occurred. The RV park owner talked to us in the office shop as we looked around for supplies we might need. We thanked her for the wonderful facilities she offered as they were better than most we had come across. Brianne washed and dried all of our clothes as we settled in for the night. It was so good to be clean, dry, and warm as I drifted off to sleep.

I left early in the morning to ride out and over White Bird Pass. I ate my breakfast in the form of an energy bar that Tim had given me. The chocolate and coconut tasted great together and provided me with the energy I was going to need to start climbing again. The road had recently been resurfaced and there was loose gravel everywhere. A sign warned motorists to proceed slowly to avoid kicking the loose stones up and into other motorist's windshields. I did not have a barrier between me and the flying stones and soon found that I would be dodging them all the way up to the summit. The morning drivers decided that they would drive as fast as they felt like and I was pelted here and there by the rocks they kicked up. The stones also made for an interesting climb as my tires slipped on them every now and then too.

The grade was not as bad as some I had ascended and so the going went well other than the barrage of rocks. It was a long stretch that climbed up to the summit but once I reached it the world opened up again for as far as I could see. I was supposed to take the old road down. The old road coiled like a snake for miles and had no traffic on it. I took the main route instead which shot straight down at a high rate of speed. I had the shoulder to protect me from most of the traffic, so I hurled down the mountain like a cannonball. It was one of the few descents along the journey that I liken to something that one reads about in a work of fiction. It really needs to be lived in order to fully experience it.

I was a little nervous that I would miss my next turn as I had gone off the reservation in terms of the route I should have taken. I stopped at the bottom next to the White Bird exit and looked over my map. It appeared that I could keep going so I continued on. I came across a restaurant on the other side of the road but was moving too fast to want to stop. I crossed two other cyclists heading the other direction at a slow methodical pace as they started to ascend the massive mountain that I had just came from. I knew they had a few hours of ascent ahead of them and wished them a safe and steady climb. I was heading down to where the river met the road now and I began to climb up and down along it through the various canyons. It began to rain on me softly and then turned into a downpour again. I was glad for the rain this time though as it was supposed to be awfully hot down there this time of year. The rain took the heat out of the air. I pedaled on through a couple of towns and got lost in the day. At one point I reached into my handlebar bag and produced an energy bar to munch on. I opened the package with my teeth as I kept on riding and took it with one hand while I ate. A part of the wrapper tore off and blew away from me onto the shoulder. I squeezed the brakes to stop before I got too far down the road and parked the bike to walk back and retrieve it. I did not want to be that guy who ruined the trash less roadside. I had seen such trash along the way here and there and could sometimes tell that a cyclist had been the culprit based upon the refuge. I thought it extremely rude as we were all just guests moving through these places.

After a good long wet and epic day of riding I came across the town of Riggins. I was in the mood for a hot cup of coffee and pedaled down the main street looking for some. There was a rafting company that appeared to sell coffee based upon their sign, so I stopped there and removed my wet over garments before sitting down to rest. A group of women started down the steps and stopped in front of the entrance to speak with their rafting guide. They were all in swimsuits and rain covers. It would be an adventuresome day to go rafting, that was for sure. While I waited for them to move down from the entrance I realized that there was not much here in the way of coffee, so I put my jacket and helmet back on before heading further down through the town. The streets became narrow and the water ran down them from the overabundance of rain. I was riding through a small stream instead of a road now. Towards the other end of town I finally came across a coffee shop and stopped in. I parked my bicycle under the overhang near some outdoor seating and headed in to order. The woman behind the counter was in the back getting fresh baked cinnamon rolls out of the oven and I waited for her to complete her task before saying hello. I stayed on the door mat too to keep from dripping all over the floor. "Oh, I am so sorry I did not see you come in." I let her know that I was just fine and that I could really use a hot mocha. She whipped one up for me. I went outside to keep the water out of her shop and sat down next to my bike. The coffee was sweet and warm as it passed my lips and moved down my esophagus warming up my core. It was a little shocking at first but then melted into a comfortable feeling. My hands were so wet that it was hard to use my cell phone's touch screen to call Brianne but I eventually got it to work. The screen kept jumping around on me as the water pooled on it. Brianne said that they would wait for me at a rest stop further down the road, so I finished up my coffee and left town.

The rain just did not let up. I was cold, soaked, and really tired. I pedaled on down the shoulder of the road and hoped I would reach the rest stop sooner than later. I passed up stopping at the next town and kept to the main road. I began to hear loud honking from behind me and turned my head to see a white pickup truck blaring their horn repeatedly at me. They kept on it until they had passed me and then a passenger rolled down their window to extend their middle finger to me. I was not sure what I had done to invite their hostilities but there it was. It reminded me of the time back in Omaha that a young man had yelled out at me from a passing car to get out of the road. He had used some choice words towards me as they sped by. I had more of a hot head for those types of people back then and I erupted into a boiling rage as I pedaled as hard and as fast as I could to catch up with them. Most unfortunately for them they got caught up at a red light behind some traffic and I was able to over take them. I can still see the look of uncomfortable fear on the guy's face as I tried to entice him to exit his vehicle to talk with me about his big mouth. He had rolled up his window and just kept looking forward most likely praying for a change in the light. I calmed down a bit and rolled off down the road. I am not saying that I reacted as I should have but that is in the past. I did not have the satisfaction of catching up to these guys and nor did I try. I let it go.

When I finally reached the rest stop I was starving and cold inside. Brianne had setup Isosceles in the truck parking lot and was cooking barley vegetable soup. I parked my bike outside the hitch and knocked before I opened the door to walk inside.

I greeted her and then quickly got out of my wet clothes while she finished making lunch. The boys were over in the camper van with my mother. I turned on the propane furnace to get my body temperature back up to a satisfactory level. The heat felt so good as I sat there with Brianne. I was dry and warm now and soon had a bowl of hot soup to add to my comfort. The boys and my mother were happy to see me and we all ate together in the camper van while Gabriel slept in Isosceles. The rain continued to fall making pitter patter sounds upon the roof as we talked to one another. Then there was a sudden boom and a shudder! We all looked around at each other wondering if a truck was running into us or something but nothing moved. I looked outside and found that a truck had run into the canyon wall across the street though. It had hit it hard and was now resting there. A sheriff quickly came and parked behind it with his lights flashing. The driver looked to be all right and he spoke with the sheriff before getting into his vehicle to get out of the rain. We went back to eating lunch. The boys let me know that it was time to use the restroom and I walked them over. The puddles were small ponds on the walkway as we crossed around and through them on the way. There was a group of travelers picnicking under a shelter to the left. We walked back to the camper and loaded everyone up. Brianne and my mother wanted me to be done for the day. There was a campground not too far from there on the route and we all agreed that it would be safer not to venture back out in this weather after the middle finger and then the accident. I was good with that, so I loaded the bike onto the new roof rack carrier we had purchased back in Missoula. It was the first time I had used it and it took me a moment to figure it out. The bike fell over a couple of times banging loudly on the roof of the

SUV but no damage was done from what I could tell. Once the bike was safely in place we hit the road to find the next campground.

We came across a town called New Meadows and stopped at the gas station to fuel up. My mother went into the restaurant and came out with five large root beer floats. We parked in the back and all enjoyed them as the sun set. We checked out the RV park in town but there was no vacancy as far as we could tell. The owner was not in and there were no spots left to park. It also appeared to be a full time residence kind of place rather than an overnight accommodation. We moved on down the road to the next turn in the route where there was a National Forest with US Forest Service to camp in.

Evergreen Camp Ground was just a ways into Payette National Forest. It was tucked away in the pines and was very primitive but had just enough room for both of our vehicles. The host stopped by to get our information as we filled out the payment forms and let us know that she was leaving for a few days. We would be on our own. I thanked her and began to set up camp. There was a stream next to our site and the running water along with the dry warmth of our home lulled me into an easy and restful slumber. It was our last night in Idaho. I really enjoyed the Northern part of the state.

Oregon

The morning started off with blueberry pancakes at mom's camper. They were so good. She had procured a bottle of huckleberry syrup to accompany them and we enjoyed the view of the forest through the camper van's windows as we ate. We all slept in and I was ready to hit the road. There was a hot canyon ahead of me once I left the National Forest and then it was on to Oregon! My bike needed some work though as my rear derailleur was not shifting correctly. It was popping in between gears keeping me from putting any real torque on the pedals. I squatted down in the entrance to the camp ground next to the empty amphitheater that by the looks of it provided evening entertainment for campers in days long ago. I looked the chain and the gears over, not finding a visual cause. I stood up, removed the panniers, loosened the rear brake cable, and then flipped the bike upside down laying it to rest on the seat and handlebars. I unscrewed the rear quick release bolt and slid it out of the hub. Once the wheel was free I removed it and then repositioned it back on the chain and in the fork. I secured the wheel and then spun it by cranking on the pedals. I tested the shifter and found it still did not align the chain with the gears correctly. I fished out my multipurpose tool and opened up the Philips headed screw driver to adjust the position of the chain over the gears. Once it was aligned I tested it again and found the shifting to be smooth. I flipped the bike back over and put the brake back in working order before running it around the entrance shifting up and down the spectrum. It was good enough for a days ride. Once everything was loaded back up I took to the road.

We were going to finish in Oregon at the end of the day and I was very happy of the prospect of being in the final state. The morning took me out of the lodge pole pined mountains and into a semiarid valley. I stopped at a gas station and purchased a large chocolate milk and some jalapeño poppers to munch on while I rested in the parking lot. There was a mural on the side wall of the place depicting where I was and the sites to see all around me. A group of bikers were reading the mural too and asked me what I was up to on my bicycle. I told them about how I had journeyed all the way there from the East Coast and they were amazed. They too loved seeing the countryside little by little as they slowly moved along it in search of great adventure. I find a lot in common with bikers out on the open road in this regard. We had fun talking about the canyon ahead and what it might look like. My family pulled up along the street just past the station and I wished the bikers safe travels as I walked my bicycle over to the SUV. Everyone was in good spirits and we all ate lunch, my second, together in the camper van. After lunch I went back into the station to buy ice for our coolers. Ice was a wonderful item to carry. It kept perishables from perishing and drinks cold enough to freeze your brain when the temperatures soared. Brianne and I had learned to keep a fresh stock of the commodity while we drove our trucks across the great Iraqi landscape during the war. There were moments where I thought our third country national drivers would have mutinied had we not provided them with ice for the day!

From there we said our goodbyes for the afternoon. I turned down the road less traveled, heading out of the gas station parking lot towards Hells Canyon. The road immediately turned into a slight grade heading up and I knew that I was in for another long end of day summit. I met an eastbound cyclist who was fresh into his second state coming out of the canyon that morning. We talked for ten minutes or so about how pumped we were to be out in God's great country living our dreams. He looked fresh still and I was happy to cheer him on. He was so excited for the journey ahead. I let him know about some must stop places along the route and of course to be pre-pared for the dogs in Appalachia. I wish I could have spent an evening telling him more about the ride ahead but he probably wanted to experience it all for himself as I would have. He told me how happy he was for me as I was about to cross into the final state of my adventure. I wished him well.

The canyon road summited after a long drawn out haul. Then it bent severely downward for seven miles of intense glo-ry. I was traveling so fast down that winding road that I even passed a car! My first overtake of a car traveling at normal speed. I probably should have taken that as a warning that I was traveling too fast for the grade and curves but I was on fire and shot down the canyon at top speed! At the bottom Brianne, the boys, and my mother were waiting for me with a hand spun chocolate milk shake. The ice cream was so delicious and I was ready to ride the rest of the seven miles into Oregon. There was a couple sitting outside in two recumbent bicycles looking up at the ascent that I had just come from when I left the store. I walked Gabriel over to the side of the lot near them to let him do his business and found them to be in what ap-peared to be a deep meditation. I did not want to stir them as I knew that they were girding their loins for the task ahead of them. I helped Brianne pack everyone up and then pedaled lightly out of the gravel lot and back onto the road.

The canyon opened up down the road revealing a surreal landscape of sharp dry canyon walls holding a large green lake between them. The late day sun turned the landscape gold and a bright light reflected off the emerald water below. I have seen so many magnificent things as I journeyed across America and this was among the best of them. I cannot imagine living my life now without having experienced all of this. The road wiggled and wrapped itself along the canyon walls and I looked out and down across the lake. Then came the dam holding back this great body of water. A net hung over the path to catch falling boulders and I rode under its shadow and out the other side. It was a hydroelectric dam and now I was near the industrial part of it. I quickly zoomed down and then out onto a bridge crossing into Oregon where this would all end in water.

My family was waiting for me at the other side of the river next to the welcome sign. I was truly and finally in Oregon now. I had crossed thousands of miles to get there. We took photos at the Oregon sign and were chased off by a swarm of bees. They must have built their hive near the sign and we were trespassing. We all lit out and headed for Oxbow where we planned to end the day. The road to Oxbow was lined with wild cherry trees, huckleberries, and many other berry bushes that I think were not as edible. I picked a handful of ripe cherries and ate up. I was not going to skip out on these and they were on the lake side of the road either way. I pocketed some for everyone else and rode on. There was a sharp climb a few miles in and it was a bit much for my tired legs and lungs. My lungs can get a little less than productive toward the end of a long hot day and that day was no exception. After the hard climb there was a quick descent into Oxbow. I turned off route at the T in the road and made my way to the RV park and camp grounds. This was a great place to camp. They had power, water, a dump station, showers, flush toilets, picnic tables, pull through sites, and loads of friendly people to chat with all around. I was a little nervous about the "run for your life if you hear the siren" signs around the place but Lord knows the dam was probably not going to give way the night we stayed over. There were only two more maps left in my set to go through and about 670 miles until Astoria. We planned on arriving on the 20th or 21st of July at that point and called to let my father know some good dates to make plane reservations to meet us there. We all went to bed clean, full, and comfortable.

The climb out of Hell's Canyon was more brutal than I would like to admit. I did have a little assist from the weather being uncharacteristically cooler than it should have been for that time of year though. The morning started out overcast and I had slept in of course. Conor and I took Gabriel for a nice long walk and then we had breakfast with my mother in her camper van. Spinach and cheese scramble with toast were on the menu and the coffee warmed me up. After all of this I finally started getting ready for the day. I had to make a few adjustments to my rear derailleur to get it to shift correctly again. It was sticking in the easier gears and could not shift out of them. I spent about 20 minutes trying to adjust things. All of this added up to me leaving really late in the morning. The weather was cool enough though and I was good with that.

The road out of Hell's Canyon consists of gentle climbing until you reach Halfway Town and then it becomes a long steep grade over a pass. There were large rocks in the road and I avoided them by keeping a keen eye out for them. After the pass I rolled into Richland where I stopped at a cafe for a huckleberry milkshake and a large basket of curly fries. The waitress told me the road to Baker City was not bad from there but I beg to differ. I do not think she had made the journey on a bicycle before. The wind pushed back at me the entire way and the sun came out in full force. I started to climb some hills which led into another canyon. A large number of east-bounders passed me in the road as I worked to keep my momentum going down the canyon into the wind. One of the riders told me that they were going across the country the easy way and I could only assume that they figured the prevailing winds would make their journey less work. Ha, there is no easier way to go as the winds come from everywhere and particularly out of the South on most summer days. Even if the winds stayed out of the West the entire trip by some strange miracle it would still be a cross wind for a good portion of the adventure. No, I think it is both hard and rewarding no matter which way you choose to cross.

The sun hid from me again and the clouds took on a darker tone. I knew what that meant having been through this before. I reached the bottom of that canyon run and began to ascend the other side. The sound of thunder echoed off the canyon walls as a light rain began to fall cooling me off even more. I had to stop and wait behind a line of cars at a construction check point while the crew packed up for the day because of the rain. I put my lights and jacket on. I was soaked by the time we all started moving again and the rain began to fall harder. Brianne passed me further on down the way and waved signaling that she would come back around. I pedaled on as she passed me again and waited for me at the next turn out. She had lunch for me and I ate it in the car. The windows fogged over from the heat my body was emanating. It was comforting to be out of the rain for a while. We debated on the merits of stopping for the day as I downed a couple of sodas. I was here to ride though and I kissed her goodbye before heading back out into the rain. There was another 25 miles left to go before I reached the city we were staying in for the night. Those miles turned out to be epic.

The storm did let up as I started out again. I dried out in about 30 minutes and was feeling great. I tucked my jacket away and enjoyed the sun. The sunshine did not last though and another storm began to pass through the area darkening the skies again. The road began to become one climb after another. As I was cresting one hill where the road passed through the dug out rocks and sand the worst storm I have ever ridden through bore down on me. The wind threatened to toss me from the road and into the mud to my right. The down pour turned to salty hail that battered my body and the lighting shot out around the hilltop followed instantly by deafening claps of thunder. I pulled hard off the road and opened my panniers to whip out my jacket for shelter from the vicious on slot. I was glad to have it as it offered up a last barrier between me and nature's full on furry. The jacket clung hard to my skin in the heavy wind. The cars and trucks blew past my as they hurried to get out of the storm. I got back on the shoulder and bore down on the pedals moving ever so slowly through the storm. Once it had passed I was left cold, drenched, and completely spent.

Lucky me, the hill I was climbing next brought my body temperature back up fairly quickly but did nothing for my exhaustion. I started to brew a headache. I had been getting some nasty ones over the past several years due to a pinched nerve in my neck and the never ending stress of my job. Now the stress of having lived through that crazy moment coupled with giving everything I had left in the tank gave me a real zinger. I kept soldiering on though up the hills and into the sunshine. I had learned to work through the pain. The hills finally ended around five miles outside of town and I found I did have some fuel left after all to finish strong for the day. I could see the next set of mountains off into the distance as I rode through the farms that surrounded Baker City. The storm was far off in the distance now and the mixture of dark and light made for a beautiful sunset.

Brianne and the boys were waiting for me at the RV park playground a mile or so inside of the city. Conor ran up to me and hugged me. I needed a hug and I might have shed a tear or two. We had pizza for dinner and went shopping for fresh fruit. I had a warm, done for the day, feeling in my body. I love that feeling. Later the boys watched a movie with my mother while Brianne updated some online media. I began to ache all over and hoped to find myself sufficiently renewed in the morning as I usually did. I had three passes to climb as I ascended into the Cascade Mountain Range the next day and that was it. The last mountain range left before the Pacific Ocean.

The RV park that we spent the night in was awesome. They had everything you could ever need to include a hot tub and a general store. It really is the little things that make me happy. I woke up well rested and lubed up my chain for the long hard day of climbing not one, two, but three passes. I was excited to push myself up and over them as I was starting to count down the number of passes left before the sandy beaches of the Oregon Coast. I left the RV park and cut across some back alleyways while I worked myself to the route. I had gotten a little turned around once I reached a main street and flagged down another morning rider who was on his way to work to inquire about which way I should head next. He was very kind and pointed me in the right direction. He had saved me a few blocks of back tracking too as I was about to head in a semi-wrong direction. I stopped at a gas station for some pass summiting candy, two boxes were on order for that day's work. I then headed over to the hot counter and picked up a bean and cheese burrito. They were truly terrible rock hard abominations out in that part of America. Every small shop carried them starting in Wyoming. They were all the same. Hard to eat but for some strange reason I was drawn to them. I liked to douse them in picante sauce and then power up on their spicy chewiness. Besides, there are not a whole lot of hot options for a vegetarian on the road. You might be thinking but hey Dan did you know that some bean burritos are made with lard? Well, I am not going to go there. Ignorance is bliss. After my burrito and an iced coffee I ventured out of the city and into the central part of Oregon.

The first pass of the day was not so bad. It did require a long hard push to get to the top though. The terrain went from rocky to treed again and this was by far my favorite type of scenery. It is usually cooler and less windy in the tree cover. They were little sanctuaries from the elements along the trail. Once I was at the top of Sumpter Pass it was a short downhill into the gap between it and Tipton Pass. I zoomed on through the part where the gap leveled out and then began to climb once more. This pass took even more time to conquer. I started to feel a bit of a wobble to my rear tire. I needed to pull over before I lost control. The tire was flat. I moved over to the side of the road and removed all of my gear. I flipped the bike over onto the handlebars and removed the rear wheel. The tire came off easily with my lever and I inspected it for the root cause of my flat. If you do not take the time to fix what punctured your inner tube you will soon find yourself fixing another flat soon after you get underway again. I had learned this well before on a taco ride in Iowa one night. I had run over a thorn that had broken off hiding itself in the tire so that it punctured my spare too after changing it out. I was walking after that and for a very long stretch. I carry two spare inner tubes with me these days and check for root causes. The current culprit was another one of those thin metal wires. They must have been part of a truck tire sidewall or something. Boy did they find a way to ruin my day as I came across them. I worked it out of the tire and put the new inner tube in place before prying them both back on the wheel. Brianne drove by as I worked and I waved at her but she never made eye contact. I had to laugh at this and gave her a hard time for it later that evening. A park ranger pulled up too while I was inflating the tire but not to see if I needed any assistance. He was there to retrieve a road sign and left as quickly as he had come. I finished the repair and got under way summiting the second pass. It ended up being a little steeper than the last pass toward the end and I was getting tired at this point.

We had planned on meeting for lunch at Bates State Park in the gap between this pass and Dixie but the road heading off the route towards it was a mean looking gravel that I had no intention of going down. I am glad for many reasons that I skipped it but the most important was that Brianne had decided the same and was not there waiting for me. There was no way for us to communicate our movements with each other since the cell phone service was incognito as it had almost always been those days. I really think that we would have been better off with a wifi only phone saving the crazy monthly amount of money that the cell phone company thought was fair for not providing service. I was low on water at this point and found a shop on my map just down the road. I drained the last of my water as I neared it and then found myself in a mess of trouble.

The shop was closed. There was no one there and the sign on the door alerted me that I had come on the wrong day of the week. It also promised huckleberry ice cream and hot food if I had come on the right day. I was crushed. I had no water, it was hot out, and I was really tired. I walked over to the shade of a tree and sat by the road eating a granola bar waiting to see if Brianne or my mother would come by looking for me. After about 30 minutes I saw my mother's camper van and waved at her as I walked out towards the road to get her attention. She did not slow down and that is when I noticed that it was not her but a couple in the same kind of camper. They waved at me and drove on down the road. I imagine they might have had some reservations about stopping for the large bearded man on the side of the road. That is when I decided that I had to climb the pass in order to get to water. There was a town on the other side that I could coast to once the hard work of summiting was over. The top of the pass also had a US Forest Service campground that might have water. Some did and some did not. I was out in the full sun as the road went straight up flanked by the forest. I crossed several little creeks and seriously considered drinking from them but put off risking getting sick. I could always turn around and coast down to them if I got desperate enough. I should have packed a filter and recommend that those who plan on riding this trail do so for times like these. I was pretty much toast by the time I reached the Forest Service side road. I stopped to catch my breath and then saw Brianne coming my way up in the distance. Our SUV was unmistakable with the bicycle rack on the roof. I flagged her down and she turned in. God I was glad to see her. She had soda, food, and water for me. I drank until I was bloated and then went for the salty stuff.

After being saved from the heat and well rested I got out of the vehicle. I moved on up the rest of Dixie Pass. The summit was not far from there and the grade really rounded out after that point giving me less trouble as I pedaled on. It felt so good to have summited the last pass of the day and I had a much deserved long drawn out descent to look forward to before the sun went down. It was getting later in the day and the sun was lower on the horizon now. I quickly found myself in Prairie City where I stopped at a grocery store for soda and an orange push-up pop. An older couple walked up to me as I sat outside in the shade eating my snack and asked me about my ride. They were out adventuring and riding around too as they traveled here and there in their RV. I had fun chatting with them and then gathered up my things and rode on out of town. The road opened up into a warm valley with farms dotting the landscape here and there. I just kept going as the pedaling was not so bad anymore on the slow descent. There were times where I had to work up a small rise but nothing like the passes I had come from. Eventually I made it into John Day where I stopped in at Dairy Queen.

I ordered a large strawberry malt and then sat down to enjoy it in the cool air conditioning. The restaurant was sparsely populated. I updated my blog using the wifi. The manager came over to see how I was doing and gave me a funny grin as she walked away. I had no idea until I went into the restroom to wash up that I had whipped cream all over my beard. I must have looked pretty silly. I filled my water bottles with ice and cold water before heading out and then waited in the evening traffic to turn back onto the route. The day felt like it had no end as I just kept moving forward toward the setting sun. I was overjoyed upon reaching the Clyde Holliday State Recreation Site where everyone had set up camp. I had a little trouble crossing the road to make the left turn as traffic had really picked up but I made it in safely.

The campground was well shaded with green grass that they watered from the time we got there until when we left. It had a stream towards the rear and a long loop of RV sites. We got to meet Joe and Gail, the couple that I had thought was my mom from earlier. They were set up in the site next to ours. Brianne, my mother, and the boys had met them earlier in the day at a train depot while exploring. Joe and Gail had recommended we stay at this campground. They ended up being really great people and later introduced us to another couple across the way who had stopped in on their way to the original Transamerica Ride Reunion in Missoula, Montana. The husband had been one of the original riders in 1976 and he showed us his memorabilia to include the original field guides that they gave the riders. We talked for a good hour and wished them a wonderful trip. What an amazing end to the day. There were showers and hot soup for dinner. The electric hookups gave us cool air until we headed to bed and then warm air when the night became cool.

The next day ended up being a hot one. I started the day with an off stomach and a headache. I was not sure if it was the water at the campground or the really long day of riding up those three passes the day before but I was in no hurry to hit the road. I took Gabriel out for a walk around 5:45AM and then snuggled with the kids until 8AM. We all had breakfast together and I started to feel good enough to head out. The first 26 miles were flat for the most part and it was 80 degrees outside. I stopped in Dayville for some snacks. There was a little gas station there with a small selection of items. I bought a box of snack cookies, candy, soda, and ice cream. I was sitting outside in the smoking section enjoying the cookies and ice cream when Joe and Gail pulled in. They asked me if I needed any water as a joke from when they passed me by the other day. I laughed and told them I was good to go. They wanted a picture of me and Joe cleared away the ash tray from the table I was at to get a good one. I smiled big and then wished them safe travels as they mounted up to head off on their own adventure. They were an awesome couple that I was very glad to have met. They recommended that we stay at Fort Robinson State Park in Astoria at the end of our journey. We followed their advice.

I poured the left over ice from my now finished soda into one of my water bottles and made sure I had packed heavy on the water for the heat of the day that was coming. I rode on to John Day Fossil Bed from there and entered a canyon before the turnoff. I slowly rolled through the shadow of the canyon walls next to a stream. It was fun to bike through such places. I passed by the turnoff for the fossil beds where Brianne and everyone else had gone exploring, to continue my forward movement. The day started to really heat up as I left the shade of the canyon. I also started to climb some steep grades that did a number on me in the sweltering temperature. I should have left a lot earlier in the day or stayed over one more night as my stomach got better but there I was. I did pass by a tree full of shoes though and found a sign at the base that stated they were a bunch of old souls hanging around. I enjoyed that and found it worth the days ride. Later down the road I swerved to miss an object on the shoulder and nearly put myself in front of an oncoming truck. I swerved back just in the nick of time and had a "come to Jesus" moment with the risks of not paying better attention to what I was doing. My family caught up with me soon after that and we all decided to spend some time in the park in the next town while the sun sunk a little on the horizon. There were a handful of RV spots next to the park but all were taken. We rested and ate lunch in the pavilion waiting an hour or so before moving on.

We stayed in Ochoco National Forest for the evening. The campground had some strict rules and no water. The camp host really got after my mother for running her generator and wanted to make sure she knew that it had to be off by 10PM. We assured him it would be. Our neighbor down the road came up to me to let me know that the host was not just picking on my mother. He had been doing the rounds with everyone to ensure they knew and upheld the rules there. He had his marching orders. I took a short nap under a large pine while the boys played. The shade from the trees created a perfect resting temperature. When the sun started to fade I got up and cooked dinner for everyone. I made shepherd's pie and the kids watched a movie with my mother. Brianne and I mapped out the remaining days of the trip and found we would be in Astoria on the nineteenth now if all went to plan. I was so excited to complete the journey but also a little sad it was really coming to an end. I had a feeling of impending loss.

The evening turned cold and I awoke extra early the next day to ensure that I stayed out of the heat. I had to bundle up before I topped off my water bottles from our five gallon reserve jug. I rode out of the sleepy campsite and onto the route heading at a downward slant to the next valley. A small fox ran across the road ahead of me carrying the hind quarter of some dead animal and then dropped it in the middle of the road upon realizing that something bigger was afoot. I rolled past the carcass holding my breath. My hands and face stung in the cold air. I kept on pedaling in the silence of the morning listening to the whir of my tires as I spun further toward my destination. I made up a little song about hash browns to pass the time and I sang it on a loop for 30 miles until I reached the next city. I got Starbucks there for the first time in weeks. I parked my bicycle right under the no bikes allowed sign and walked in. The mocha I ordered could have been better but it was hot, caffeinated, and sweet which did the trick. It was a rare treat to be in a heavily enough populated area to find one of those shops and I left there in search of egg, biscuits, and some hash browns of course. The McDonalds down the way did not disappoint. I doused my meal with salt and then smothered it with ketchup to ensure I had enough sodium for the day. I was in heaven to have had such a great breakfast and left elated. I rode out of the city and then out into the countryside. I started to see the Cascade Mountains far off into the distance and smiled broadly to have caught a first glimpse of the last mountain range of my journey. I was a little shocked to be overtaken by another rider as I was talking loudly to myself. I had gotten into the habit of doing so since I was out in the middle of nowhere for days on end without a soul in sight. The man startled me and he chuckled as he powered by me. He had no panniers, heavy tools, or gear to weigh him down as he rode around the area for pleasure. I still laugh a little as I recall the moment putting myself in his bicycle shoes. He must have thought oh Lord I have to pass this huge, dirty, bearded man who is talking to himself in the middle of nowhere where no one can hear my calls for help! Ha, that is too funny.

The rest of the day's ride took me through the backroads to my last base camp before my last pass. I rode past an old ghost town where there was a blockade in place on the road leading up to it warning people not to enter. A rusty water tower loomed overhead and I was curious but ever forward was my motto. I popped a spoke as I turned down another backroad and a couple stopped to make sure I had everything I needed to repair it before they drove on. I crossed paths with a woman who was at the very beginning of her journey having just completed her first mountain range. She was fresh and ready for anything as she ventured forth into the unknown that was this adventure across America. The route eventually turned off onto the main highway and then ended up in the town of Sisters. I had a head wind for the last several miles but a spectacular view of the Cascades.

I rode through a sea of traffic down the main street. I had missed my turn and stopped for Ice cream at a parlor called BJ's. "Strawberry malt please!" I exclaimed when it was my turn to get some hand dipped goodness. I walked across the street from there into a farmer's market and waded through the crowd exiting the other end on a side street. I rode passed some shops and then a neighborhood before turning back onto the route. There was a sign that told me I was on my way to McKenzie Pass. I was soon in a dense forest and came across the campground we had said we would meet up at. Brianne was there waiting for me but the place was full. My mother had gone up the pass to find another one and we waited for her there in the shade of the old ponderosa pines. She returned to report that there was also nothing ahead for miles. We took another drive around the loop to see if there was a new opening and by God there was a large pull through site that we all could fit in that had just became available. We parked, paid, and set up camp. Aaron and Conor played in the dirt and then ran up and down the forested hill side. We rested awhile and then asked my mother if she could watch the boys while we went into town to celebrate our long journey.

We stopped for coffee at Sisters Coffee Company, hit the farmer's market, and then had dinner at Rio on the side of town where I had entered earlier in the day. After dinner it was BJ's ice cream for dessert. Mint chocolate chip for me this time. We headed back to camp with pints of ice cream and happy as could be. The evening was very cold after the sun had set. So cold that I turned on the propane furnace to fight back the frosty air that had settled in the camper while we slept. The furnace made me comfortable enough to drift back to sleep as I listened to the soft snores of our children and Gabriel.

I woke up just before the sun began to rise. I quickly gathered my gear and made sure the bike was ready for a morning of climbing. I had a granola bar and an orange for breakfast as I rolled out of the campgrounds. I passed one site which had set up road signs they must have collected from various places along their way. I found them entertaining and a little odd but I have set up wacky things as well around the office when I worked in information technology. I could see my breath in the air and I had to make sure I was bundled just enough to not sweat or become numb. The road tilted slightly up as I worked through the ponderosa pines on my way to the pass. I passed a controlled burn ahead sign and was happy to see that it was not taking place at that moment. The next sign warned RV travelers to turn around as they would become stuck on the pass should they attempt to make the tight and awkward turns ahead. Then I was turning up and along the mountain side heading into a steep grade. I stopped to rest in the silence of the morning and then continued to work on the ascent. At one point the road emerged from the forest into a windy open area where I could see for miles across an old lava field. The wind was chilly as it worked through the openings in my jacket. I zipped up some more to protect myself and sat there looking out over the scene. It was really something to behold all by myself. I rode on and crossed the Pacific Crest Trail. I had now crossed both of America's really long through hike trails that run north to south. The path was now running next to giant lava rock that encroached upon the road. This was why RV's had needed to seek an alternate route. I knew Brianne would be all right though as Isosceles was only 19 feet long. I remembered this spot from one of the YouTube videos I had watched about a man who rode the same direction as I had on a recumbent bike a couple of years before.

The real view was just ahead though as I crested the summit. The road was now flush with most of the lava field and you could see the largest peaks that comprised the cascade mountains all around. I was the only one up there as it was still early and the sun was just on the horizon. The wind and I shared a moment as we meditated on the stark contrast of the place to all others we had both traveled during our lives. It was just amazing. I was filled with such awe at the treasure that this moment was. After a long pause I took a picture of my bike next to the pass sign and then looked over the stickers that other cyclists had placed on it as they had come through before me. I saw the TransAmerican Race stickers from this year and the one before. I saw many others from riders who have personal logos they leave behind along the way. I had made it up my last pass of the TransAmerican Trail. I was going to head down to the coast from there. Down from the chilly black and snow capped desolate landscape through a rain forest that ended in the salty spray of the open water.

The rest of the day took me into a greener forest with heavy undergrowth. I started to cross signs alerting me to the thousand foot drops in elevation as I zoomed and zagged down the tiny winding road out of the mountains. The traffic began to pick up as hikers and tourists came to explore. I felt overwhelming joy as I journeyed down. I ran into a strong headwind as I came out of the mountains and had to battle it as I climbed up and down through the foothills. I came upon a wedding on the backroads nestled in an orchard. Further down the road their reception was set up and awaiting guests. A handful of guys were smoking meat and the air was filled with hardwood and campfire notes. I began to lose my head of steam as the afternoon stretched on and stopped at a grocery store to pick up some chocolate milk and one of those bean and cheese burritos I had been finding everywhere. I rested outside as I feasted and watched people come and go from the bar across the parking lot. There were two fully loaded road bicycles outside of the door and I did consider heading in for a drink or two but ever forward. I finished out the day on the backroads that passed near the City of Eugene and headed into Coburg where there was an RV resort my family had set up camp in. They were swimming in the pool as I rolled into the resort. I could hear Aaron's delight as he slashed around in the water. I rushed to the camper and changed into my swim suit. I secured my bike and hit the showers to clean the dust from the road off my body before jumping into the pool and letting the soreness of my muscles melt away into a more relaxed state. I tossed the boys up into the air and they came down with a splash. We had a lot of fun. Brianne did our laundry while I entertained the boys and then we all headed into town for dinner. We found a friendly place that served short order along with pies for dessert. My mother treated and the boys even had some of her steak. We were celebrating the upcoming end to such a wonderful journey together. We all slept so well that night.

I was traveling north again the next day. I rolled out of the RV resort nice and early as I knew there was a McDonalds right up the road over the interstate. I stopped in and waited in line to order. A young woman, who must have just started in the fast food industry, keyed my order in incorrectly and the manager kind of laid into here in front of me. I am not big on managers doing that in public as corrections should be either constructive and positive or done in private when warranted. I let the manager know that everything was really all right. That I was going to get what I had ordered and paid for and I was in no way, shape, or form upset. I took my food over to the table farthest from the counter to eat in peace. Another rider rode up and parked his bicycle next to mine before coming in and giving me a nod on his way to the counter. He came back about five minutes later and placed an overflowing tray on the table. He was much smaller than me and was about to eat twice what I was. He was from Switzerland and heading westbound as well. He had mountain bike rims and did not move at the same pace as my hybrid rims allowed for. We both knew that I would slip away quickly as we left that place and so we talked for a good stretch. We had plenty of coffee and discussed everything we had been through along the way. How good it would feel to swim in the ocean and put the bikes away. To truly rest. We shook hands and congratulated each other on a job well done before heading off into the late morning. I lost track of him about a mile later and never saw him again.

There was a foot race going on in town and I came upon the stragglers as the others had already jogged off my route. They were out enjoying the morning too and I thought of how much fun it would be to participate in a race like that if we lived there. The going was easy as the roads were flat in that area. I was in farm country again and the climate was pleasant. I passed by blueberry farm after blueberry farm and they were in season. The bushes were heavy with blue bundles of sweet berries. Brianne picked up a large quantity of them up at the store and they are truly no better anywhere else I have ever had them. I could travel to Oregon just for the blueberries each July when they are ripe and ready to be devoured. I pedaled on and passed an east-bounder on a recumbent. He was not in the mood to stop and so I kept going. There is a lot to take in on the first state of the ride and I imagine he was busy with making sure he was going the right way. Either that or I was looking wild by now. I had noticed that the restrooms out this way had become off limits for even customers at most places. I learned quickly to ask first and then purchase where I was welcome to wash my hands before eating anything. No sense in getting ill this close to the finish line. The day was overcast and pleasant. I did find a public place to use the facilities and wash up near a very small town.

I spent almost the entire day pointed north and then came upon a large road that had an onramp with a sign that stated I could take this way to the coast! I was on a westerly collision course with destiny now. It was a long haul though in heavy traffic. I made full use of the shoulder to stay out of the dangerous parts of the road and crossed a casino as the sun was starting to set. I met Brianne and my mother in a parking lot in the next town and we searched for an RV park to stay at. We found one further down the road and I pedaled on to meet up with them there. It ended up being mostly for permanent residence but we did find one open spot. After pleading with the host we were allowed to park my mom's camper van in front of our camper and make it fit. We ran off the 20 amp and she got the 30 amp service. A woman stopped by to ask me what I was up to and I let her know. She invited us over to her mobile home for drinks but I told her we needed to eat, clean up, and get the kids in bed. Our neighbor to the right was there working a temporary job and we spoke of places we had both been through the screen window on his RV while I made supper. He had lived in Alaska for a long stretch and I let him know we too wanted to live there to explore the vast wilderness up north. I prepped the bike for an early departure and then we walked down to the creek to stretch our legs before bed. There was a woman with a small child sleeping down there and we left after a short time so as not to wake them. We nestled in for the night excited for the first glimpse of the ocean that was to come the very next day.

I left early and pedaled on through the morning until I found a coffee shack next to my turn onto Old Historic Highway 101. The coffee was good and I sat on a bench as the sun rose higher into the morning sky. Everything was green around me and the air was fresh and just the right temperature. The sun felt good on my face and I thanked the woman in the shack before I headed on my way. Her yellow Labrador wagged his tail at me as I departed. The next thing I knew I found myself in a berry enchanted forest riding through the soft morning rain. The rain came down in a mist that got me wet but failed to soak me. It made the green forest around me even lusher and the berries really stood out. I was out there all alone on this old road that time had forgotten and I moved up its slight grades and dodged questionable riding surfaces as I made my way closer to the coast. I could have skipped this old way and gone straight to the ocean but I liked the tease it provided.

The forest gave way to a brighter coastal treed area as I came through the last off the hills between me and the ocean. It took around ten more miles and then I saw it. I was high above it and it would be several more hours before I got to the first beach but I was there! I pulled into an overlook and parked. I jogged to the stone wall that stood between the public and the steep drop off there after. I pulled out my chips and bean dip and sat there on that rock wall just watching the waves come in for a good hour. There were some beach homes down below and a few people walked in and out of my view. I was finally there. That is when I felt like my journey had really come to its conclusion. The rest was just going to be my victory march up the coast to Astoria from there. I had done it. I had crossed the entire country taking the long way through every National Forest, Park, and Monument along the way. I had summited more passes than I could remember and conquered the most significant mountain ranges that America had standing between east and west. I was really there and this was really happening.

Brianne, the boys, Gabriel, and my mother showed up and we celebrated! Overcome by emotion we took it all in and shared that shining moment of triumph together. Then it was on to Tillamook for ice cream and cheese curds. It took me three hours to get there as it was a long way up the coast. I rode along the coastal road from beach to beach and ended up climbing some very large hills as I went. I rode right into a cloud which was whipping up the coast as it blew in from the ocean. I have always wanted to know what it was like to pass through a cloud and now I knew. It was a unique experience that I highly recommend you seek out. I went down from there out of the clouds and found myself on a rocky beach where I rested on a boulder and watched two woman dig, for what I believe were clams, in a patch of sand. I was exhausted at this point. My body had been thoroughly run down from the constant demands I put on it every day since leaving the Atlantic

Coast and now it was unraveling. I had a sore throat and a cough. I just needed to rest.

Tillamook was further down the road and I passed some logging operations complete with large log trucks creating interesting riding conditions. The city was busy and the cheese factory ended up being on the other side of town. I pulled in just as Brianne had gotten back to the campers with the most amazing cheesy goodness. There were curds, grilled cheese, fries, and loads of ice cream. Sometimes when I share my journey with others this cheese comes up in the conversation towards the end and you can tell who has been out this way by the way their eyes just light up at the mention of Tillamook. We stayed there for a long time. Then it was on to an RV park off the coast in Brighton. My mother and the boys had fresh crab boil and Brianne and I had sweet corn as we watched the sun set over the ocean. Our campers backed up to a patch of blackberries and our view from the front door looked out over the water. What a magical and restful place to lay my head down after so many days on the road. I slept well through the night and I knew the next day was to be the last on my bicycle.

The morning was really a victory ride. I went through coastal towns as the sun rose and watched people enjoying life on the ocean as I glided past. I saw Haystack Rock and got to ride up some big hills that spilled out over ledges with killer views of the Pacific. I then passed into Seaside where the TransAmerican Trail traditionally ends in the cold blue water of the Pacific Ocean. I got off my bicycle and walked along the boardwalk to the ramp that headed down to the sand. A woman asked me where I had ridden from and she looked at me with shock and disbelief as I replied, "Virginia on the

TransAmerican Trail." She smiled and walked on down the beach. My family came running up to me led by my beautiful wife Brianne. We were just ecstatic as we drug the bike across the sand out to the ocean to dip the front tire into the surf. Conor put sand in my gears to complete what Aaron had started 66 days ago on the beach in Yorktown. I was not worried as I knew that it would work itself out as it always had. What an experience and one I will take with me to the end of my days. We walked into the surf together and the boys and I stood up to the crashing waves, all was well with life.

Later I rode the traditional last short haul of the ride into Astoria and was treated to a few more steep hills along the way. A Chihuahua chased me for a half mile just four miles from the end. He was mean but I warned him that a truck was going to hit him if he did not get back onto the side walk and he gave up the chase. The evening was spent on the beach at Fort Stevens State Park overlooking an old ship wreck and watching the setting of the sun. Gabriel ran in and out of the ocean which shown golden in the last light of day. The bike, now dormant on the roof of the SUV, rested. I was with my Family.

Chapter 5

The Long Way Back Home

We headed up the coast to Washington to see cousins who had visited with us a long time ago as they passed through Omaha on their way to the West. They were into getting their kids outdoors, had adopted the same vegetarian lifestyle that we had, and so we found much common ground. After sharing a meal and exploring a park with them, we headed to meet my mother at an RV park in Portland near the airport. It was a full time residence kind of place and we had to park along a cement wall. It was warm out and we did our best to stay cool until the sun began to hide low on the horizon late in the evening.

My mother and I left together to pick my father up from the airport. He had taken a flight that had a transfer at one point and that was when the computer systems at the airports failed causing massive delays across the country. He ended up getting in really late and everyone was asleep upon our return. He was not well adjusted to living in a camper van and was in a hurry to get on the road the next morning heading back to Omaha with my mother. We all had breakfast together and said our goodbyes. I am so thankful for the time we were able to share with my mother over the summer. You only have so much time on this earth and spending it with loved ones just beats about everything else you could be doing.

After that we were on our own again as we had been for the first leg of the journey. We drove down the coast and checked out Crater Lake National Park. It had to have been the bluest water I have ever seen or will see in my entire life. There was snow on the side of the road as we wound our way up to its rim and the adventure of the place really took ahold of us. We stayed in a US Forest Service campground later that evening and met a woman who was out on the road exploring America with her large German Shepherd.

We traveled down further south and into the Redwood National Forest where the trees were both ancient and large enough to live inside of. I just had no idea that trees could grow that large until we walked among them. We found a wonderful RV park along the coast that was foraged by a heard of Elk in the mornings and late evenings. We hiked the area and ate wild blackberries before turning in for the night. We explored the forest for another day and then moved inland the next.

From there we cut across hot and mountainous desert terrain as we moved into Nevada. We stopped for an oil change at a national chain store and unfortunately watched as they ripped my bicycle off the roof as it exited the garage. I was saddened by the damage and rough treatment of such a good friend. It took them months to settle with us but I guess they made us whole again. From there we drove all day and into the late dark night twice before making it to Salt Lake City, Utah where we met up with some old friends who had moved there many years ago. Our kids played together in the neighborhood splash park before we shared a couple of pizzas back at their place. We left there full, happy, and a little sleepy as we drove again into the dark of night making it to the first rest area in Colorado before stopping. We set up Isosceles to catch a few hours of sleep and then moved on again in the morning.

We stopped in Palisade to buy peaches and boy was it worth it. I can still taste those tree ripened flavor explosions. We bought a flat of them and headed up to Frisco but the interstate was closed due to a rock slide. We ended up detouring through Aspen and then over Independence Pass. This pass was practically one lane for the most part and it took us a very long time to summit. The view from the top was just amazing. I was glad we had to detour through there. We met back up with Aunt Kathy and Uncle Don a lot later in the day then we had anticipated. They took us out for Mexican food and we talked their ears off about the last half of the journey. We settled in at our favorite camp ground by Lake Dillon and said our goodbyes before tucking the boys in for the night. The next day we descended from the Rocky Mountains and out onto the high plains of Nebraska before driving late into the evening where we ended up safe and sound in our own drive way. Home sweet home.

The kids went straight for their toys as we opened the garage door. You could tell that they were overwhelmed with the joy of being back from the road. We had made it. All that was left to do was get life back in order and find employment before we ate through our savings.

Brianne and I spent the next several weeks clearing the forest that had risen up around our home while we had been away. Our river birch trees had grown all the way to where their lower branches touched the ground. The thistles were taller than me out back by the garden and I had to take them on one at a time. The boys started first grade and we settled back into life in a stationary home. I had a great deal of trouble finding a suitable replacement for my old work, so I started a consulting business providing Information Technology Services in the area. I also cleaned restaurant ceilings late at night and into the morning hours to afford groceries. Brianne took on three jobs and we still do not earn enough to clear all of our modest bills each month. We are very rich in what matters the most to us though. We have been so blessed to have so many free hours with the boys exploring, helping them with school, and taking them to our favorite fall pastimes. Brianne worked for a local pumpkin patch and the boys and I went out to enjoy the fruits of her labor every day between September and October. We picked apples in the orchards and feasted on Thanksgiving with family. It is the Winter Solstice now and soon we will celebrate the return of longer days but most importantly the birth of our Lord and Savior Jesus Christ the light of the world. May God bless you and keep you on your journey.

Daniel McDonald